Ken
GOODMAN

On
Reading

HEINEMANN
Portsmouth, NH

Heinemann
A division of Reed Elsevier Inc.
361 Hanover Street,
Portsmouth, NH 03801-3912

Offices and agents throughout the world

Published simultaneously by Heinemann in the United States
and Scholastic Canada Ltd. in Canada.
First printing 1996

Cover design by Terence Kanhai.

Cataloging in Publication information is on file at the Library of Congress.

Printed in the United States of America
98 97 96   IMP   1 2 3 4 5 6

 This paper is acid-free and contains 85% recycled product
and 15% post consumer waste.

This book is dedicated to Yetta Goodman
who has traveled the journeys of my life with me as lover, wife, friend, counselor,
co-conspiritor, interpreter, colleague, challenger, and organizer.
She has lifted me up when I've been down
and kept my feet on the ground when I might have become too full of myself.
There is no idea in this book that has not been shared with, interrogated by,
contributed to by Yetta.
Her parents named her Yentela, her students dubbed her Meta Yetta,
our University calls her Regents Professor.
This book is for her.

Acknowledgements

I acknowledge first those who have contributed to this book: Caryl Crowell, Fred Gollasch, Debra Goodman, Yetta Goodman, Wendy Hood, Mieko Iventosh, Prisca Martens (and her daughter Sarah) and Kathy Whitmore.

Next I want to acknowledge the "miscueteers," the many former students and colleagues who collaborated in my miscue research, and Yetta Goodman, Carolyn Burke and Dorothy Watson, who extended the methodology of miscue analysis into forms available to teachers in the *Reading Miscue Inventory*. I should then also acknowledge hundreds of readers of all ages who read for us, presenting wonderful miscues for me to use in developing my theories.

Next I want to recognize the linguists Michael Halliday, C.C. Fries and Noam Chomsky, the psychologists Jean Piaget, Lev Vygotsky and Jerome Bruner, and the philosophers John Dewey and Susan Langer, whose work I've drawn on in building my own perspectives.

I've had more direct and continuous personal contact with another group of scholars whose work I've drawn on: Louise Rosenblatt, Harold Rosen, Margaret Spencer, Frank Smith, Brian Cambourne, Roger Shuy, Robert Ruddell, Richard Hodges, Paul Kolers, Harry Levin, Emilia Ferreiro, Marie Clay, Don Lloyd, Peter Fries, Steve Strauss, John McInnis, Garth Boomer, James Britton and E. Brooks Smith. No scholar exists in a vacuum and my professional associations with these colleagues have given me opportunities for the discourse so necessary for developing ideas.

Many journal editors and the program planners for IRA, NCTE, NRC and other groups have provided opportunities for me to share my insights as they were developing. Members of the Center for the Expansion of Language and Thinking have been a particular source of support and useful criticism.

Adrian Peetoom has been the editor of three of my books, including this one. He and Fran Buncombe at Scholastic Canada understand what I want to say and help me say it better than I could myself — and in less space.

Finally, I need to thank the many teachers who welcomed me into their classrooms and who shared with me not only questions about my ideas but also stories about how they've used those ideas in their teaching.

Contents

1

*The sense you
make of a text does not
depend first of all on the marks
on the paper. It depends
first on the sense you
bring to it.*

What is reading?

Right now, as you begin reading this book, I ask you to take a moment to examine what it is you do when you read.

We've probably never met, and yet you can look at the marks on this page and have the sense that you are seeing through them to the meaning I was representing as I wrote the words. How do you do that? Think about it: I wrote the first version of this introduction at a computer in my home office on an April 1993 morning in Tucson, Arizona. At that time my text existed as *ideas* in my head, as *active memory* in my computer, and as *hard copy* produced by my laser printer. Since then it has been rewritten, edited and published. The text you are reading, some years later and perhaps a long distance away, looks quite different from the one I wrote that day. Yet you and I are communicating through it. How?

In creating my text, I was putting meaning into writing, working hard to make my ideas sensible to you, my intended audience. So is it my meaning, precisely, that you are encountering as you read this page? Not really, because communicating meaning isn't that direct. In reading this book, you have to take your turn at trying to make sense of it. ("Make sense" is a common way of saying "construct meaning.")

You are *trying* to make sense of what I have written, my published text — that's the important point. However hard I work to make my text sensible for you, you can't escape the work of making sense of it yourself, of constructing your own meaning. I can't simply project my thoughts, understandings or meanings into your head. No matter how carefully and cleverly I write, no text of mine will ever "contain" my message so precisely as to guarantee that I communicate my exact "intended meaning" to you and every other reader. Each of you will construct your own meaning, employing your own values, understandings and experiences as you do so.

In fact, as each of you transacts with this published text, you will construct a parallel text in your mind and it is that text — your personal text — that you are comprehending. I, the writer, have constructed my text; you, the reader, are constructing yours. Your reading is as active and constructive a process as my writing. Moreover, each time I edited it, I reconstructed my text, and each time you reread it, you will reconstruct yours. Reading and writing are both dynamic, constructive processes.

I'm not suggesting that the kind of text I construct is unimportant in our communication. As a writer, I'm conscious of my audience. I try to construct a *real* text, one shaped by the linguistic conventions of written English, conventions of orthography, grammar, word meaning and text construction. And I try to create a *sensible* text. I begin with meaning and construct a text that, at least potentially, you can make sense of. A random list of words and punctuation marks is not authentic text.

I must confess that what I asked you to do in the first sentence of this chapter was a bit of a trick, since it implied that you could learn about reading by looking at how you, yourself, make sense of print. Then I showed that reading is a *constructive process*, and if you think about it, that fact leads to two conclusions:

➤ No two readers will ever produce the same meaning for a given text.

➤ No reader's meaning will ever completely agree with the writer's meaning.

Actually, we've got to focus on the nature of language first, before we begin examining ourselves as readers and writers. You can't understand what reading is about without focussing on words and letters, but I wanted you to think about the process first. Right from the beginning, I want to undermine any tendency you might have to think of reading as the "simple" act of recognizing letters and/or words, and to do that I have to stress two important points:

➤ Texts are more than collections of letters and words.

➤ Making sense of texts involves complex control, by both readers and writers, of how language works and how texts are constructed.

As I'll say again and again throughout this book: *the sense you make of a text depends on the sense you bring to it*.

I also want to help you to understand how it's possible that, even with the great amount of research and writing that has been done on these topics, so much misunderstanding still exists about reading and about written language in general. I believe that this confusion exists largely because people have started in the wrong place, with letters, letter-sound relationships and words. We must begin instead by looking at reading in the real world, at how readers and writers try to make sense with each other.

I haven't really tricked you. I've only started you thinking about *reading as a process of making sense from print*. Actually, that's a pretty straightforward thought, and I'll try to make the book equally straightforward. I'm conscious, however, that some of you may never have questioned some widespread misconceptions about reading that may interfere with your making sense of the logic of my view and the evidence I present for it. To anticipate your concerns, I need to explain how large bodies of research on reading have arrived at wrong and counter-productive conclusions. I'll try to do it without wandering too far from my objective of being straightforward.

Fortunately, I have two powerful tools working for me: your own experiences as readers and the experiences of those people, mostly children, I've worked with over the years. The first I've already employed in asking you to examine your own reading, and I'll do more of that. In fact, at a number of points in this book I'll ask you to involve yourself in some experiments in which you'll be both research*er* and research*ee*. (Yes, there is such a word. I just made it up.)

I will also provide several authentic examples of what readers actually do as they read, gleaned from many years of research on the reading process. Using miscue analysis, I've come to understand what readers of many different ages, levels of proficiency and language backgrounds do as they read real whole stories or other real texts. Their unexpected responses — what I called *miscues* — have given me a window into what was going on in their heads during their reading. As I've often said, everything I know about reading I've learned from children, since most of my research has been done with young people as they develop as readers. In this book their reading will help me to share with you what I've learned.

My background

Mistakes have to be part of the process of making sense of print.

That's a good cue for me to explain, by summarizing my own learning about reading, what gives me the right to write this book. You'll notice that I don't talk about degrees, awards and honors, although I've received my share of those. My purpose is to allow you to judge the view of reading I present not by who you think I am, but by whether you can test what I've learned against the reality of your own reading and that of readers around you, both in and out of your classrooms.

I first began to focus on understanding reading while I was a doctoral student at UCLA in the early 1960s. Two factors sparked my interest. First, I wanted to understand the process well enough so that I could help teachers help children become effective readers. Second was my encounter with the science of linguistics, which made me aware that reading had not yet been studied as a *language process*. As I combined my interest in reading with my interest in linguistics, I became convinced that studying *reading as language* would reveal a good deal about the process.

I diligently searched the professional literature, expecting to discover that I was not the first to reach this conclusion, but I found almost nothing. Leonard Bloomfield, the foremost linguist of the 1930s and 40s, and Clarence Barnhart, of dictionary fame, together wrote a series of short workbook-like materials based on a kind of linguistic phonics for the US army, but they hadn't studied reading.

So, with a fresh Ed.D. and an assistant professorship at Wayne State University, I set out to study reading as a language process. That is, I wanted to treat reading as the written language counterpart of listening. Literate societies use two forms of language, oral and written. Each form has productive and receptive aspects, as the diagram shows.

Language processes		
	Oral language	**Written language**
Productive	*Speaking*	*Writing*
Receptive	*Listening*	*Reading*

To study reading as receptive language, I knew I would have to observe *real readers* reading *real texts*. Otherwise, I wouldn't be examining the complete language process. Although the conditions I set for my research may seem logical, even self-evident, they did not and do not characterize most reading research. In general, experimental reading researchers have carefully reduced the research tasks to a few controlled variables. Most reading research has involved asking readers to read phony texts in highly constrained laboratory circumstances. Steven Rose, a neurobiologist, points up the problems of this kind of reductionist research into memory and brain functions:

> . . . to adopt a reductionist methodology in research strategy — that is to stabilize the world that one is studying by manipulating one variable at a time, holding everything else as constant as possible — is generally the only way to do experiments from which one can draw clear conclusions. Error comes in if one over-interprets the relevance to these conclusions, by forgetting the artificial constraints of the experiment and instead assuming

that in real life, outside the laboratory . . . such changes involving a single variable can actually take place; that it is a simple matter to extrapolate back from the artificiality of laboratory isolation to the complex, rich interconnectedness of the real world. (Rose, 1992, p.210)

Reductionist research in reading has inevitably focussed on recognition of bits and pieces of language rather than on comprehension of real texts. But we can't assume that perception of letters and words in the process of making sense of real meaningful texts is the same as recognizing letters and words in isolation or in highly reduced contexts. And we can't assume that comprehension follows successive recognition of words.

So I got permission to work with first- to third-grade children in a racially and economically mixed urban school (Goodman, 1965) and learned how to study reading as it happens in the real world. I asked the children to read orally an unfamiliar, moderately difficult text so I could study what they did as they read a text for the first time. I wasn't sure what I would discover as a result of this deliberately uncontrolled reading task, but in the end what caught my attention most was the *miscues*.

Every child's reading varied from an accurate response to the print in some way. They made mistakes — that was no surprise. But what wonderful mistakes they made! Even with my limited knowledge of linguistics (I learned a lot on the job), I could already see that these young children were operating as experienced users of language. Unlike most other researchers, who assumed that mistakes reflected incompetence, inexperience or carelessness, or some combination of these, I discovered that *mistakes are part of the process of making sense of print*.

My young readers weren't just sounding out or recognizing letters and words. They were making sense, and to do so, they were combining language cues from the printed story with what they knew about how language works. I quickly came to the conclusion that the children were using the same cues in the unexpected responses as in the expected responses. That suggested to me that an appropriate term for the mismatches between what the reader did (observed responses) and what I expected (expected responses) might be "miscues." It seemed like a much more positive word than "mistakes" or "errors."

What follows are two examples of children's miscues from that very first study:

Brian:

Jimmy said to the man, "We will

    a

find the little monkey."

a

"Find the toys," said the man.
"And we will find my monkey."

Brian substitutes "a" for "the" at two points. Notice that he has already read "the" successfully.

Vanessa:

the

"Let us go to a big park this year," said Sue.

Vanessa goes the other way. She reads "the" for "a" in two places.

the

"To a farm," said Mr. Parker.

At first, I often made the reductionist error of looking for simple cause-effect relationships, single causes for each miscue: this an omission, that a dialect miscue, another a grammatical error (as in "a" for "the"), still another a semantic problem. At the time of these examples, my joy came simply from finding the children substituting determiners (noun markers) for determiners, clearly using grammatical information. Many years later, however, I did an extensive study of miscues on determiners and discovered that these children had actually demonstrated much more language sophistication than I had thought, changing definite to indefinite noun phrases and vice versa. To do what they did, these six-year-old readers had to control, on a deep intuitive level, the English noun system. They showed this control in their miscues.

Once I understood that readers use all kinds of cues at the same time, I had to develop a *taxonomy of miscues*, a way of analyzing each miscue at several levels and in several aspects. As my research extended to readers of varying ages, cultures and proficiency, the taxonomy became more complex and my colleagues and I became more sophisticated in our understanding of the reading process.

I also realized that, although traditional linguistics was helpful, I was really researching how readers make sense of written language, and this involved both language and thinking. Clearly, reading needed to be studied as a *psycholinguistic process*.

With great trepidation, I presented my first findings to the American Educational Research Association in 1964. (I still remember the question Jeanne Chall asked me: "How do you explain that your readers sometimes inserted words in their oral reading that weren't in the text?" I don't remember my answer.) The chair of my session, the eminent language educator Dr. Nila Banton Smith, suggested that I send my paper to *Elementary English* (now *Language Arts*, a journal of the National Council of Teachers of English), which published it in 1965.

Just as an interesting aside, although that first study laid the foundation for many years of miscue research, it was an incidental experiment within it that has attracted the most attention over the years and caused the paper to be labeled, in one anthology, "a classic study." I had made lists of words from the story, which I asked the children to read ahead of time. I wanted to test the belief, commonly held among teachers, that children can read words in stories that they can't identify from lists, and I found overwhelming support for that belief. Even first-graders, in reading the story, could read two out of three of the words that they couldn't identify in the lists. By third grade, the proportion was up to four out of five. My explanation was that in reading the story they could draw on both semantic and syntactic contexts, while in lists they had no cues other than those in the out-of-context words themselves.

When the article appeared, most people responded, "So what! I knew that." Yet, for me, that incidental experiment confirmed what miscue analysis was teaching me about the reading process: reading isn't recognizing words, it's making sense of print. It was only when other researchers sought to challenge my developing view of reading by focussing on this finding, however, that my paper acquired its "classic" status. I find that humorous. What started out too obvious to be important became too important to remain unchallenged.

Back to my story. That first AERA presentation turned out to be important in other ways. Helen Robinson, professor at the University of Chicago and a long-time associate of William S. Gray, suggested that I become a member of the new joint NCTE-IRA Committee on Linguistics and Reading. Jeanne Chall, who had recently become a professor at Harvard, gave my name to Harry Levin, a developmental psychologist at Cornell University, who had just received a major grant from the US office of education to study reading. So, in the summer of 1966 I spent a month at Cornell working with an interdisciplinary group of researchers and theoreticians, a golden opportunity to bounce my developing views off people with very different perspectives, among them Harry Levin and psychologists James and Evelyn Gibson.

Noam Chomsky, a brilliant linguist from MIT, also visited us for three days. The timing couldn't have been more fortuitous for my research. In his presentations he characterized reading as "tentative information processing." This idea of tentativeness — using current information but remaining receptive to conflicting information — was a missing link in my understanding of reading. I went home from Cornell and wrote the article "Reading as a Psycholinguistic Guessing Game" (Goodman, 1967), in which I transformed Chomsky's "tentative information processing" into "psycholinguistic guessing."

As readers use cues from the linguistic text, they bring their knowledge and beliefs about the world to bear on making sense. They 'guess' what's coming, making predictions and inferences; they are selective about use of text cues and they monitor their 'guesses' for contradictory cues. Effective reading, then, is not accurate word recognition; it is getting to meaning. And efficient reading is using just enough of the available cues, given what a reader brings to the reading, to make sense of the text.

For the next 15 years I engaged in very intensive miscue research. In one study, I looked at a full range of readers from second to tenth grade, at all levels of proficiency: low, average and high. In another, I studied eight populations of American children: four who spoke low-status dialects of American English (rural black, Appalachian white, downeast Maine and Hawaiian pidgin), and four second-language groups (Navajo, Samoan, Spanish and Arabic). The miscues of those readers helped test and refine the miscue analysis taxonomy, as well as a new model and theory of reading I've been developing. It's true that everything I know about reading I learned from children!

I wasn't alone, however. Many colleagues and graduate students engaged in these and other miscue studies. Doctoral dissertations have used the large data bases the major studies generated to explore many aspects of the reading process. Hundreds of articles and research reports using miscue analysis have been published. Miscue studies have been conducted on reading in many different languages including Spanish, French, Polish, Yiddish, Hebrew, Portuguese, Chinese, German, Japanese, Greek and American Sign Language. In this book, "we" used in connection with research represents a large community.

My wife, Yetta Goodman, first with Carolyn Burke and later with Dorothy Watson, developed the *Reading Miscue Inventory* to give teachers a way of understanding and evaluating their students' reading. It's widely used in English-speaking countries in teacher education programs and reading diagnosis. Versions have been developed for French and Spanish as well.

In another direction, many teachers and scholars (myself included) have used the miscue data bases to look at the nature of written English texts and how text features influence reading. My miscue research focussed on the reading process and not specifically on how children learn to read or how they should be taught. However, my reason for wanting to understand reading has always been to inform teachers so they can understand more precisely what it is that children are learning to do and how best to help them. I've also written extensively on language curriculum and teaching, using my insights into written language. My research and theory have even been used in the study of how children develop literacy.

If my work has been influential in the whole language movement, it's because my research has always involved real learners and real books. Teachers don't need to take my findings on faith; they can test them out with their own students in their own classrooms, with little effort or cost. Many whole language teachers over the years have used the concepts not only to understand their students but also to develop sound, effective instruction. And, in turn, I've learned, and continue to learn, from what I see informed teachers achieve with empowered learners. That will become clear in the final chapter.

Some thoughts about reading

In spite of diversity within, reading is a universal psycholinguistic process, a single way of making sense of written language.

When I began to study the reading process, I often heard two directly opposite positions. Some conference speakers would begin by saying, "Since nobody knows how reading works . . ." and follow it up with some sort of justification for a kind of trial-and-error approach to reading instruction. Other speakers and writers would imply, or actually say, "Everybody knows how reading works . . ." and then make it appear that the only possible way to teach reading was *their* way. These positions actually held back progress in coming to understand the reading process. What's the use of research if we can't know or already do?

My position has always been that the process of reading, however complex, is knowable, and that the scientific study of reading is both necessary and possible. My purpose in this book is to bring together what has been learned, up to this point, through the scientific study of reading by carefully observing readers (including ourselves) in the act of reading. I don't claim to understand reading fully, but I do contend that we know too much to say "nobody knows," or not to use what we already do know. Fortunately, there are now a large number of teachers who know a lot about the reading process and who are putting that knowledge to work in their classrooms. And in doing so, they are producing more knowledge.

One final thought about the universality of reading. My own research has been limited to reading in English, but I'm convinced that there's a single reading process — just one way of making sense of print — regardless of differences in language and orthography.

French readers will predict that adjectives will follow nouns, of course, and German readers will expect verbs at the ends of sentences. Japanese readers will scan print from top to bottom when it's presented that way, while Hebrew and Arabic readers will scan from right to left horizontally and infer vowels when they're not marked in the print. My students, and others who have observed miscues in other languages that use both alphabetic and non-alphabetic writing, provide plenty of research support for my belief in a universal model of reading.

I offer two related reasons:

➤ The constraints of the semiotic system of written language make it necessary for all writing to produce graphic shapes, organized and arranged on a surface so they can be perceived and comprehended by readers. What particular form the system will take can vary considerably, but all forms must be producible by writers and perceivable by readers.

➤ All writing systems must be useful. Form not only follows function; function also shapes form.

So what we find is diversity within the unity of a single socio-psycholinguistic reading process — a single way of making sense of written language.

Summary

This, then, is a book about how *reading* works as a process — or about what readers do when they read, which is the same thing. I'll also have to consider *writing*, of course, and the nature of written text, since readers transact with texts created by writers. And, since reading is a language process, I must pay some attention to the nature of *language* and the relationships between oral and written language. But my focus will be on reading and readers.

I'll confess up front, however, that I may take the opportunity now and then to point to the implications of insights on the reading process for reading development and instruction — it seems inevitable. Still, except for a summary in the closing chapter, this is a book on reading and not on reading instruction.

2

*Oral and
written language
are both real language; they
serve overlapping
purposes.*

What is language?

Until a few decades ago, language scholars paid little attention to oral language, perhaps because it's so ordinary, so all around us. Generally, written language tends to be used for the more sedate and elegant language functions, while oral language is used for all kinds of things, some of them quite mundane, even vulgar. (Not that you can't be vulgar in written language, of course!)

Then linguists, quite correctly, shifted the focus. They pointed out that oral language comes first and is used a lot more by most people than written language. However, this new direction led to a problem: the misperception, now commonly held, that written language is a secondary language form, not only because it's learned later but also because it's not "real language." Some popular and professional terminology reflects this view, implying that written language is just a way of recording speech, which is the *real* "real language." For example, "sound-symbol correspondence" implies that oral sounds are not symbols while written letters are. A lot of research wrongly assumes that written language must be re-coded as oral language before it can be understood. A scientific-sounding term for phonics is "decoding," which holds a similar implication: that written language is code but oral language is not.

But my research on reading and my synthesis of the work of others lead me to believe that written language is neither less nor more important than oral language. Written language isn't just a way of representing oral language: it *is* language every bit as much as oral language is. Oral and written language processes work in much the same way, and they are learned in much the same way. In this chapter we'll look at how written language and oral language are alike and how they serve overlapping purposes and functions.

In literate societies, the two language forms are parallel. In oral language, speakers produce sounds and listeners perceive those sounds through *hearing*. Oral language is used primarily for face-to-face, immediate situations, when speakers and listeners are within reach of each other's voices. Facial and body movements are also part of the visible context that shapes and defines oral language.

Written language uses graphic shapes on flat surfaces, and readers use *vision* to perceive these shapes. When people need to communicate beyond the reach of their voices in space or time, they invent written language. Literate people can send their writing over great distances, to be read and comprehended by other literate people perhaps long after it was written, even long after its author has died. Written language is, therefore, a means of storing and passing on the culture to future generations.

Today's information society would collapse without written language, even with all the electronic communicating devices we've created: telephone, voice recording, radio and television, movies. Computers and fax machines require written language, and there's a copy shop on almost every business corner replicating thousands of printed documents. Little CD disks can store whole encyclopedias, combining oral and written language, and still and moving pictures. Written language can be "printed" on a screen or on paper by a printer.

The characteristics of language

We must see everything in language in its relationship to meaning.

Language is a human personal-social invention. Individuals, in social groups, invent and develop language because they are capable of symbolic thought. That is, they can let symbols represent experiences and ideas, which they can then reflect on. Humans are also born dependent on others for survival, and they remain interdependent throughout their lives. It is this combination of symbolic ability and social need that makes language universal across human societies.

But language is not just a collection of symbols; it is a *system of symbols*, a semiotic system. It has to be a system because it not only names things, actions and experiences, but also represents the way all these interact in all the subtleties of our experiences with each other and the world.

Oral language

Oral/aural language ("oral" for mouth/"aural" for ear) uses *sounds* as symbols, and those sounds occur only in *syllables*. Since we can't produce strings of uniform distinct sounds, nor can we hear them, we speak and hear syllables instead. One or more oral syllables compose a *morpheme*, the smallest unit of language that can carry part of the meaning or grammar. A word may include one or more morphemes, and one or more words form a phrase, a word group or a clause. These are found in sentences, dialogs, texts. (For more on this and some of the following sections, see my *Phonics Phacts*, 1993.)

But make no mistake, language is not like a salami that can be sliced thin or thick, with each piece retaining all the characteristics of the sausage. If we dissect language, we kill it as a dynamic entity. In any linguistic sense, each smaller unit exists only in the larger ones.

Oral language is multi-layered. We can talk about the sounds of a language and its syllabic structure, and about its wording. But it's the grammar of the language that makes it possible to produce meaningful speech. Even so, we can produce beautifully grammatical speech that is nonsense — comedians do it all the time. Language exists only to express meaning, and we must understand that listeners (and readers) can make sense of language only if they bring meaning to it. We must always see everything in language in its relationship to meaning.

There is one group of people, the deaf, for whom oral language is simply not functional. However, deaf communities have developed highly sophisticated and efficient manual sign languages such as American Sign Language (ASL), a visible language that serves all the language functions. ASL isn't a code for oral language but a language in its own right. The symbols are hand signs, which serve as ideographs. And the grammar is spatial, using space and the direction in which the signs are made. This development of a visible language by those cut off from speech clearly shows that language and speech are not the same thing. Those who cannot hear are fully capable of inventing and using language.

Written language

Written language shares all the characteristics of oral language except that it's visual rather than aural. We use a system of graphic symbols — patterned marks — on a two-dimensional surface. These may be pictorial representations of an experience or idea, but most are more abstract than that. Characters, individually or in combination, may represent things (icons or pictographs) words (logographs) or ideas (ideographs), or they may represent the sound system of the oral language (syllables, alphabet).

Even when written language does represent oral language in some way, it also represents meaning. It's not only possible but efficient for readers to go as directly as possible to meaning, without going through the oral language to get there. As you read this, you have the sense of "seeing through" the print directly to meaning, because your perception of print, like your perception of speech, is controlled by your need to make sense.

Oral and written forms of a particular language (English, for instance) share wording, grammar and meaning. If differences occur, it's because different functions are in use or because the two symbol systems impose different constraints. Written language tends to be more formal than oral language, and that influences grammar and word choice.

However, there is overlap: formal oral language in speeches, for example, and informal written language in notes and diaries. Written language also seems more formal to us because we don't often think about things like phone messages, personal notes, billboards and signs as written language. Actually, since oral intonation helps to clarify complex clause sequences that written punctuation can't handle, the grammar of oral language is often *more* complex than that of written language.

One argument used against considering writing as language is that no human society has ever been discovered that did not have an oral language, while there are some, even now, that have no written language. Oral language appears first in human societies because it serves here-and-now functions. But there are limits to voice communication. Written language develops when oral language is insufficient for meeting the language needs of a society.

Even societies that appear to have no written language may use graphic forms to communicate. We tend to overlook some of the forms used in non-European traditional cultures because they are not alphabetic and not used for the same functions that industrialized societies use writing for. The sand-painting of the Navajos, for example, is a highly intricate process for controlling the spirit world and the forces of nature in Navajo culture. Sand-painting is so powerful that it must be destroyed once it has served its purpose.

Because speech is not very useful across time and over space, people have devised various ways of extending oral/aural communication. Some societies have developed elaborate drum signals for transmitting a limited number of important messages. Mountain people in Europe and elsewhere use yodeling to communicate from mountain top to mountain top. In biblical times, rams' horns sounded from the hilltops to initiate festivals and call citizens to arms, and conch shells served the same purposes for the Polynesians. In the Moslem world, holy men call the faithful to prayer from minarets, as church bells do in the Christian world. Sailors at sea use whistles to communicate aboard ship, while foghorns warn them of danger in the water.

Written language becomes necessary, however, when societies and their cultures spread out and develop in complex ways. When a culture needs written language, it invents it. Sometimes a written language is invented almost from scratch, but more often an existing writing system is adopted and adapted to fit the needs of the culture.

Religious missionaries have often introduced an orthography to a culture that didn't have one as a means of making holy scriptures and prayers accessible. The Cyrillic alphabet, used in Russian and other Slavic languages, was adapted from the Greek alphabet by St. Cyril and his fellow missionaries. European languages are written with the Roman alphabet because the early Christian churches used Latin. Many cultures embraced the Arabic alphabet when they accepted the Moslem religion. Jews used the Hebrew alphabet to write other languages they came to speak: Yiddish (a Germanic language) and Ladino (the variant of Spanish that Jews spoke in Spain). The Wycliff Bible Translators, a modern group of religious linguists, have dedicated themselves to developing writing systems for cultures without them.

Written language differs in its use from country to country and culture to culture, depending on how much literacy is needed and what it's used for. In industrialized societies, the need for universal literacy is only a few generations old. The monks of the middle ages were literate on behalf of their societies, copying and storing books and recording important events and documents. Even today, in many third-world countries, public scribes sit at tables in the villages and great cities, reading and writing for their neighbors.

Individuals and societies are literate to the extent that they need to be, which explains the town scribe in developing nations and the photocopy shop on so many corners in industrial nations. New forms of language emerge as societies need them. When oral language is inadequate for the needs of the culture, written language develops. And both oral and written languages develop new forms to meet new functional needs.

It's important to keep in mind, of course, that the alphabetic form is not the only existing form of written language. Computer technology has reinvented the use of pictographs and icons to represent meaning. A single easily understood icon may represent a whole sequence of actions. When I click on the ☎ icon, for example, my computer activates the series of commands needed to open my modem, and ⌛ tells me to wait while my computer does what I told it to do.

Now let me bring all this back to a central premise of this book: *reading is language, no less and no more than listening is language*. People learn both in the same ways and for the same reasons. And making sense of written language is very much like making sense of oral language.

The functions of language

Some years ago a psychiatrist colleague in the College of Medicine asked me to help him with an article on why people read science fiction. It occurred to him that it would be useful to know why people read at all, so he could put their choosing to read science fiction in a broader context. Helping him answer his question made me realize that understanding reading depends on understanding why people read: what they are trying to accomplish through reading, what functions it serves for them. For example, people read science fiction for pleasure, but they also share with other science fiction readers a fascination with what might be, with the complex imaginary worlds science fiction writers build.

I suggested earlier that societies develop written language when social needs for using language go beyond face-to-face and here-and-now functions. The same is true of individuals. We become readers and writers because we have functional needs that require us to read and write. Usually the functional need precedes the development of control of the form. Because form follows function, language is easy to learn when it's functional and very hard to learn when it's not.

Linguist Michael Halliday (1985) calls the routine uses of language the "goods and services" functions. He has examined language functions very closely, both as they develop and as they occur, and, in his view, language development depends on the development of language functions. The grammar and structure of language derive from the social functions it serves. Understanding language, oral or written, begins with understanding what people are trying to *do* through language.

In any case, to understand how oral and written languages work, we must understand what people do with them.

A mini-study

I'm going to do a small-scale ethnographic study here, which I invite you to duplicate for yourself: I'm going to look at my own reading to categorize its *functions and purposes*. I use both terms, since they have different (though related) meanings. My *purpose* will be quite specific, my *function* broader and more general. My purpose is personal, my function more likely to be shared by my society or culture.

I read the newspaper almost every morning. Newspapers are multi-functional and I have several purposes for reading them. My reading plan reflects my priorities:

➤ I like to start with the front page and the news section. But since that's where my wife likes to start, too, I often simply look for specific information — how the teams or athletes I follow performed on the previous day, for example — and move on to find the details elsewhere.

➤ I find the sports section and look for stories about the events that interest me, going to the box scores for specific information. These are usually on a separate page from the stories and in much finer print. My purpose is quite specific; the function is informational.

➤ After I find what I'm looking for, I scan the rest of the sports section, check out the headlines and read parts of several stories, though rarely a whole one. My purpose is less focussed. Since journalists know most people aren't likely to read an entire story, they give basic information early and follow with detail for those who care to know more. I might follow a sports columnist, but my hometown paper doesn't have one I enjoy. That suggests another function: in addition to information, reading the newspaper also gives me a certain amount of pleasure, a calm way to start my day.

➤ Next, I often search for the stock reports to see how the few stocks I own have done. I'm not a big "player" and I don't do a lot of buying and selling, but I feel I should know how much I've lost or gained — on paper, of course. Again my purpose is specific. I go right to the stocks I follow, paying little attention to any others. The newspaper organizes the information tabularly in small print so they can present a lot in little space, and only on Saturdays are the highs and lows for each stock included. (As I get older, I need stronger and stronger glasses to read the stock tables!) Rarely do I read any other part of the financial section, although if my few stocks have swung wildly in value, I may look for a story that offers an explanation.

➤ I usually start reading the main news section by turning to the editorial pages. What a smorgasbord of print! I must confess that the political cartoon and the *Doonesbury* comic strip, which for a long time my paper put on the editorial page, get my attention first. Here I also find the national and local columnists I follow. I'm selective, of course, usually picking those whose viewpoints most closely match mine and whom I find both entertaining and informative. I appreciate style and humor, and I like columnists who provide special insights or a different slant on the news. I read others only when they are dealing with a topic that interests me. Some I avoid entirely, if I don't like what they say or how they say it. Whether I read the editorials and the letters to the editor depends on how much time I've got and on what catches my attention. I'm in charge of what I read in the newspaper and I don't read what I don't want to read!

➤ Now I'm ready to read the news and features sections, including the ads and comic strips. I turn the pages sequentially, note headlines, read part or all of a story as my interest is piqued. Sometimes I go back to look for the headline of a story I want to know more about. I often skip ads entirely, even whole-page ads. I read them only when I have a specific interest: what's on special for the next time I shop. (This contrasts with the way I read computer magazines, which I buy and read specifically to look at the ads.) My reading of the comics is recreational and selective. Those that deal with children and schooling often serve an occupational function for me: I clip some with clever "comments" for use in my classes or my lectures.

As this little ethnographic study has revealed, I read the newspaper for many purposes and to serve many functions. I invite you to do a similar study on yourself or others. Pick a weekday and a weekend day and list everything you read. Then decide what your purpose was and what language function was represented. You might use the following form — I've filled in some of my own reading as examples to get you started.

Reading Event	Purpose	Function
Read labels on pill bottles	Identify correct pills, check on dosage and warnings	Informational
Read other labels: shaving cream can, toothpaste tube	Select items for use	Informational
Read bread labels, cereal and food cartons	Select for use in making breakfast	Informational
Read the newspaper (as above):		
Sports scores and other specific information	Get specific scores, check performances	Informational, recreational
Stock reports	Check stock performance	Informational
Editorial pages	Read specific columnists, cartoons, editorials	Informational, recreational, occupational
News pages	Find out what's happening, look for information about on-going news events	Informational, recreational, occupational
Comics	Amusement, follow on-going narratives, look for clever examples	Informational, occupational
Read gauges in car	Check gas, speed, radio dial, etc.	Environmental, informational, occupational
Read street signs, etc.	Handle traffic, get to work, avoid accidents	Environmental, informational, occupational

If you listed *all* of your reading in the above study, you may have been surprised at how much reading you do and for how many different purposes, and by how truly embedded reading functions are in life in our information-age society. If you compare your reading with mine, you'll find differences and similarities, of course, but in general we can classify the functions of reading into five main categories.

Environmental

Environmental print is all around us and we're often not even aware that we're reading it.

Informational

We all read for information, everything from labels to newspapers to encyclopedias. But we don't all read the same sources of information. Even those of us who do read the same things — newspapers, for example — vary in how often, how regularly, for what purposes and in what order we read them.

Occupational

Today virtually everyone engages in occupational reading. Office workers read memos, letters, manuals, computer screens. Cooks read recipe cards and food labels. Mechanics read gauges, parts catalogs, service manuals. Builders read blueprints, nurses read notices, bureaucrats read forms.

Recreational

Most of us also read for recreation; we simply find it a pleasant way to spend our time. What pleases each of us will vary greatly, however. We read fiction for the excitement of a story and the enjoyment of splendid language. Some of us read recreationally only when circumstance make other leisure pursuits impossible: on planes, in waiting rooms, at beauty parlors and barber shops. Even those who, as a rule, enjoy reading great fiction may prefer a detective story or magazine on a flight, or use science fiction as release from mundane workdays. Some choose romances or mysteries when they're on vacation, *People Magazine* at the doctor's office.

Many of us choose reading over other recreations, and may even join discussion groups to share our book pleasures with others. Despite the doomsayers, indicators show that recreational reading has increased dramatically in recent decades. A study comparing habits in 1970 and 1988 shows much heavier use of libraries and more reading and purchase of books by both adults and children.

Some people get great pleasure from reading what others read only for information: cook books, travel guides, biographies, even research reports.

Honest, on rare occasions I find a research report or a professional journal article an exciting and aesthetic experience. (Louise Rosenblatt, in over fifty years of work on readers' responses to literature, observes that readers read both *efferently* and *aesthetically*. By "efferently" she means for information, by "aesthetically" she means for feeling. Both may occur in the same reading.)

Ritualistic

If you attended a religious service during your mini-study, you will have experienced the ritualistic function of reading. In this kind of reading, which is often oral and responsive and sometimes in an ancient language, participation is more important than comprehension in the usual senses of that word. It brings the religious community together in a shared spiritual experience.

Summary

Human beings use language for a variety of needs. Oral language serves many of those needs, but when communication must span time and space, various forms of written langauge develop. Oral and written language are both real language, which serve overlapping purposes. Although written language has many functions and forms, in reading and writing we must always see those in relationship to meaning.

3

*Regardless
of their real and
apparent differences, written
and oral language are both
language in the fullest
sense.*

How language works

Let's come back to a key understanding: *our ancestors invented language because they needed it for thinking, learning and communicating.* In this chapter I want to explore how you and I and human society continue to invent new language forms for new functions and new purposes, a process that's much the same for both oral and written language. Language can't stay the same because we and the world we live in are always changing. We keep inventing new forms of language to do new things with. And as we change the ways we see our world, we change the language we use to express our views.

How function shapes form and genre

The *form* language takes depends on the *functions* it serves and the situations in which it occurs. A *genre*, whether written or oral or both, is a language form that develops within recurring social-cultural situations to meet the constraints of the speech acts or literacy events that commonly occur in those contexts. The aspects common to a particular genre include the circumstances and settings, the participants and their relationships, and the language constraints imposed by the situations.

The examples below demonstrate some forms oral and written language can take within specific genres.

A phone conversation

Medical Receptionist: Good morning, Dr. Gupta's office. This is Lupita.
    How may we help you?

Me: I'd like to make an appointment to see the doctor.

MR: Are you a regular patient of hers?

Me: Yes, my name is Ken Goodman; that's G-o-o-d-m-a-n.

MR: And what will doctor be seeing you for?

Me: It's a follow-up to an earlier visit.

MR: Let me check her appointments, Mr. Goodman. (pause) Doctor has an open appointment in three weeks on Thursday, May 15. Could you come in at 3:00 p.m.?

Me: I was hoping she'd be able to see me sooner than that.

MR: Is it an emergency?

Me: Not really, but the doctor asked me to check back with her sometime this week. Is it possible that she could see me sooner?

MR: I see. Well, if you don't mind sitting a while in our waiting room, perhaps doctor could manage to squeeze you in on Thursday afternoon after 4:00 p.m.

Me: That would be wonderful. Thank you so much for your help.

MR: Oh, you're very welcome. Have a good day. Goodbye.

Me: You have a good day too. Goodbye.

This is an example of the telephone conversation genre, in particular between strangers in a business context. In fact, it's an extension of another dialog genre, the conversation between a patient and his or her doctor. The *purpose* of this speech act is to make an appointment with the doctor through her receptionist. The broad *function* is conversational.

There are some "rules" that cover this genre, established by pragmatics and politeness. The language is somewhat formal and indirect ("I'd like to . . ., I was hoping . . ., Would it be possible . . .") and formulaic ("How may we help you? . . . Have a good day.") The conversation has to be short, since a medical receptionist's phone is a busy one, but it can't be shortened by eliminating the polite aspects; in fact, if the participants are acquainted, some "small talk" may be required. Dr. Gupta is referred to impersonally as "the doctor" or "doctor." And, of course, "see" has a special meaning in this genre: it means "meet with" and/or "examine."

Let's briefly look at the concept of genre in this context. People usually use the telephone for making an appointment with their doctor. The patient spells the name, aware that the receptionist may have difficulty hearing it clearly on the telephone. The doctor-patient relationship requires a certain deference from the patient, even toward an assistant. Doctors control when they see their patients (perhaps that's why they're called "patients"!), and patients choose their phrasing and syntax carefully to achieve their purpose within the constraints of a brief conversation.

A theater ticket

A theater ticket is also a particular type of a more general ticket genre. Although theater tickets have to be small (sellers don't want them to take too much storage space, and buyers want them to fit in purses and pockets), they must also contain a considerable amount of information, usually on only one side to avoid handling problems: theater name and address, date, title of the presentation, perhaps author/performer names, cost, section and seat number, serial number. The name of the printer or the sponsoring group and a union label may be included as well. Furthermore, most tickets have two halves that are separated when the ticket holder enters the theater. The same purpose could be met by punching, stamping or collecting the tickets, of course — there are usually choices in the form the genre takes and the choices are arbitrary.

The size and placement of text depends on the importance of the information, but the options are limited since patrons, checkers and ushers need to find information quickly and easily. If the ticket has two halves, only certain information has to be printed twice: seat number and date in particular. The union label might be too small to read, but the seat number needs to be easy to see even in artificial light. The point is, we read a ticket differently than we do most text: we seek out the information we need and ignore the rest. It's easy to see that the form of the theater ticket genre results from the constraints created by its use.

Field, tenor and mode

Theater tickets relate to the common circumstances, settings and situations of theaters. Halliday (1985) refers to such things as seating arrangements, performances and schedules, pricing and selling, etc. as the *field* of the genre. The field of the telephone conversation I recorded earlier would include personal health, doctors, their offices and use of time, etc.

The participants in literacy events involving theater tickets are the producers, sellers, theater patrons, staff and performers. Halliday calls the relationships between these people the *tenor* of the genre. Relationships between participants are quite important in literacy events and may strongly affect a particular genre. Tickets of different prices may be printed in different colors, and the price paid may affect how buyers are treated by sellers and staff. Choice seats may be reserved for reviewers, sponsors, friends or relatives. And it certainly makes a difference whether tickets are in great demand or sold at reduced prices to fill the house.

The choice of language Halliday calls the *mode* of the genre. Theater tickets use a printed-ticket mode, but other modes could just as well respond to the field and tenor: different kinds of tickets, some other form of receipt or token, or even an electronic list checked off as customers enter and take their seats.

Most of us handle many genres routinely, but when we step out of our routines we often discover how complex genres can be. The terse language and specialized abbreviations on a theater ticket may make it hard for even experienced readers to read if they are inexperienced theater goers. They may not understand the concept of reserved and pre-assigned seats, for example. On my first visit to a race track I was surprised to find that my "general admission" ticket didn't entitle me to a seat.

The form a genre takes may be culture specific. When Yetta and I visited a niece who had been living in Japan for six years, she wanted to take us to a performance of the Japanese opera. Although she and her husband had mastered enough Japanese for their routine lives, getting tickets became a real problem. She thought she had purchased advance tickets for a weekend matinee, although all she was given at the time was the receipt. She assumed that she would present this receipt at the time of the performance and receive the tickets, but it turned out that paying and getting tickets were separate processes. Not only didn't we have a reservation, there wasn't even a matinee performance that day!

Tickets for sports events look much like theater tickets, so are they the same or a different genre? The stub on some sports tickets is called a raincheck, and there's no counterpart to that in theater tickets, unless the event is outdoors. Airline tickets are governed by international convention, but that doesn't mean they all look the same. Some airlines combine the ticket and boarding pass; some use the ticket envelope as the boarding pass; some have moved to computer-generated tickets that include specific information like the passenger's name. Some tickets are actually booklets, with a sub-ticket for each flight segment. Some low-cost airlines have dropped tickets altogether, relying on their computer reservation records instead.

On a recent trip to Spain we found our way to the right bus terminal on the Madrid underground, bought our tickets for a trip to Toledo and back (they looked more like cash register tapes than printed bus tickets), and then enjoyed breakfast before heading out to catch the 9:30 bus, quite proud of ourselves. But after we had boarded the bus, we discovered that our tickets were for assigned seats at 9:00. We had to get off, get our tickets revalidated and take the 10:00 bus — an express, as it turned out, that got us into Toledo at the same time as the earlier one would have. Only after we understood how the system worked could we see all the pertinent information printed on the ticket. Incidentally, the driver tore a bit off the top of the ticket to cancel it.

It's clear that genres vary according to their field, tenor and mode, and that they grow out of social-cultural language uses. Members of language communities create them, and they control them through their specific participation in the speech acts and literacy events that occur in the genre. We learn to use and understand the forms of the genre as we participate in speech acts or literacy events in which the forms serve a personal and social function. I'm very good at reading airline tickets because I use them a lot (even so, I missed a connection once because I confused the flight number with the departure time), but I'm not so good at Spanish bus tickets in Madrid.

In the course of learning to talk and understand speech, we learn a variety of genres necessary for communication. As Halliday says (1977), we "learn how to mean." That is, we learn how to understand and make ourselves understood in a variety of recurring social situations. Children learn how to ask for things, how to express discomfort, how to take part in conversations. They learn how narrative works and how to become storytellers. They learn to cope with the genres important in their culture.

As societies and people mature and become more complex, written language genres are invented and learned in much the same way as oral genres. Individuals become part of the literacy club, as Frank Smith puts it (1986). They join social and cultural communities that produce various written genres and learn to use those genres to meet their new needs.

Sometimes forms become so conventionalized that they take on a reality of their own and we don't even know why we use them. Why do we sign letters "Yours truly"? Why do we say "Goodbye" when we leave and "How do you do?" when we meet people? Tradition! Tevya said it in *Fiddler on the Roof*. Tradition is vital in human society. Conventions provide a framework of easy familiarity for speakers and listeners, writers and readers, and therefore facilitate communication. When forms fail to keep up with the changing functions they serve, however, they need to be modified or new forms need to evolve to replace them. Both social *conventions* and personal and social *inventions* are part of human language use.

Oral and written genres

As I observed already, written language develops when a society needs language to go beyond immediate situations, for preservation and communication over time and space. Letters, notes and legal documents are good examples. We write notes to people sitting next to us in school, church or other gatherings when talk would be impractical or impolite. Letters share certain purposes with talk, and for a long time letters replaced talk for long-distance communication. Then telephones made talk over distance possible and they in turn have replaced a good deal of letter writing in our modern society. Now fax and e-mail have begun to replace telephone conversations for many purposes. So we've gone from letter writing to voice transmission to the electronic transmission of letters — just when some people were proclaiming the end of letter writing.

Fax is useful when the document itself, not just the information, needs to be communicated. One distinct advantage of written language over oral is the relatively permanent record it produces, which is why written language forms tend to be more fixed. Many legal transactions require written forms with precise inclusions and characteristics. The law recognizes an oral agreement but is much more comfortable with a written one, partly because the specific written language has legal definition, is written into law.

People, individually and collectively, continue to create new language needs and develop new genres to serve them. I said that form follows function, but it's also true that new forms lead to more inventions as people see potential for new uses of new forms. Computers began as ways of processing numerical data, but their potential for storing, processing and transmitting natural language led to word processing, desktop publishing and many other uses. Computer bulletin boards started as a means for group conversations on topics of common interest, originally how to use certain equipment or software programs. But they've expanded to become a means for shopping, sharing software, playing games, accessing information, handling investments, planning travel, and on and on.

Written language can also present large amounts of information in easily accessible forms like tables, charts, lists and registries. Genres are created with suitable forms for storing and organizing the information. Phone books, for example, are usually organized alphabetically by the subscriber's last name, but it would make no sense to organize a trip itinerary alphabetically.

Sometimes written and oral language genres overlap. A speech or lecture may cover the same content as a written article on the topic, and have a similar purpose. Even so, there will be differences in the two genres, since the relationships among the participants are different: speakers and listeners are in the same place at the same time but writers and readers are not. And the modes impose different constraints on the genres. A speaker may need to include a handout or use an overhead transparency, for example.

If all of this seems overly technical, don't worry about it. I simply want to demonstrate that written language and oral language are both language in the fullest sense, more alike than different even though their differences are more obvious.

The following diagram demonstrates some of those similarities and differences:

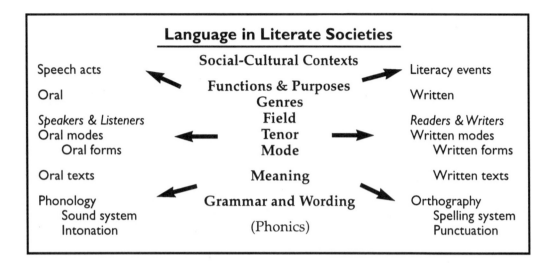

Both forms of language are authentic only in social-cultural contexts. Every authentic literacy event or speech act takes place within a genre, a social pattern created to serve a particular function and set of purposes. All literacy events and speech acts share the basic characteristics of language: field, mode and tenor. Each draws on the same system of personal-social meanings. They also share a common language structure (grammar) and vocabulary (wording). Oral language uses a system of sounds while written language uses a system of characters or letters, but they are parallel processes in every sense. Each is a complete system to serve the functions of its users in a wide range of genres, some oral, some written and some served by either or both oral and written language. And both forms of language are invented and learned in the same way.

Authenticity

The question of authenticity, especially for written language, is important enough to warrant a short word here. Each genre has its field, tenor and mode, and within an authentic literacy event, the language text that's created is also authentic. But take it out of its proper event and it becomes inauthentic. To make sense when we read, we must know the context of the situation out of which the print arises: where and when it's occurring, who's involved and what their relationships are, why the language takes this mode. A literacy event is authentic only within a situational context and a genre.

We can make sense of what we read if it has this authenticity. That means that, as readers, we have a function and a purpose for reading. It means that we bring to the reading past experience with the field of the text and with the mode in this context, and that the tenor between writer and reader is one that makes communication possible. If the genre is unfamiliar, given enough experience with other authentic literacy events, we can learn to make sense of what we read. But if we meet texts or fragments of text out of context — decontextualized language — we can neither comprehend nor learn to control the genre.

Language in literate societies

Language features become a social convention only in an environment of shared social meanings.

Language is both personal and social. We talk because we have listeners; we write because we have readers. We always write or speak in a genre, and that genre assumes both personal and social meanings.

The shopping list

I like to use **the shopping list** as an example because it's a written language genre that serves a routine purpose — almost everyone makes one at one time or another. Yet shopping lists are very personal, partly because writer and reader are often the same person, and partly because the form of the list depends on a number of personal, social, economic and demographic factors.

When I was a child my mother sent me to the grocery store with a list organized by food type: fruits and vegetables, canned goods, cereals and breads, meat, dairy, etc. The clerk behind a counter filled the list from shelves inaccessible to me. Because my mother wrote it for the store clerk, not for me, she tried to make the list explicit and complete:

2 lbs. of good medium-size Jonathan apples
6 large navel oranges (no spots)

But she warned me not to get cheated (and scolded me if I did — anyway, and I didn't *want* to get cheated), so I had to read the list too.

My own *shopping list* has some things in common with my mother's, but there are a lot of differences. My refrigerator is several times as large and much more efficient than hers (she still called it an "icebox") and I own a large freezer as well. More important, grocery stores have been replaced by SUPERMARKETS and SUPER SUPERMARKETS, which carry a stupendous variety of products arranged in bewildering arrays and tempting displays within my own easy reach.

My shopping list starts as a list on the refrigerator door — the almost universal family communication center in North American homes. Just before I shop, I usually reorganize the list with a map of the store in my head. I often write on the back of an envelope or some other handy scrap of paper, and since I'm the only reader, I use invented abbreviations. Sometimes I can't remember what I was abbreviating but, to be honest, I rarely look at the list while I'm shopping anyway — although I may check it when I think I'm done to see if I've forgotten anything. (This isn't the only time I write things I don't subsequently read. Often, the notes I take during lectures are simply to focus my attention and highlight key points in my mind.)

The list is a common written genre. Oral lists exist, too, but they're always short because they're hard for the speaker to remember and hard for the listener to follow and comprehend. However, in traditional societies oral lists often serve important purposes. In Micronesia (which means "tiny islands"), young boys learn a chant that lists island names in a certain geographical order. (Some girls learn it as well, although the culture doesn't require them to.) If they then find themselves on an unfamiliar island, they can figure out their location by learning its name and reciting their list-chant. Here's a story told to me by a school administrator who is a native of Yap:

> One day a canoe loaded with men from one island was caught in a storm. When the storm was over they found an unfamiliar island and went ashore. But the natives would not tell them the name of the island, so the men had to stay there. Over the years they married women from the island, raised families and became accepted as part of the village. One day one of the men was up in a tree collecting coconuts. His wife, swimming in the lagoon below, called out saying, "Isn't this island the most beautiful in the ocean?" They began to argue, and inadvertently she blurted out the name of the island. The man climbed down from the tree, called his friends and, using the chanted list to locate themselves, they went home.

Written lists have several useful qualities:

1. They organize specific information so that readers (and writers) can remember or access it easily.

2. They exhibit particular aspects of the information:
    (a) They might be ordered chronologically (historical events, steps in a process, class schedule).
    (b) They might be ordered by such things as size, cost, rating.

3. They present information in a logic order, by categories and sub-categories of relationship.

4. They order information hierarchically. For instance, this list assigns numbers to one level of information and letters to subordinate information.

5. They provide quick, direct access to particular information:
    (a) through numerical ordering (account numbers);
    (b) through alphabetic ordering (phone books, dictionaries);
    (c) through other relationships that can be expressed linearly (levels of cost).

Each kind of list responds to a specific human need. While dictionaries and phone books are useful organized alphabetically, an alphabetic shopping list would drive us bananas (pun intended). However, I can imagine **THE AUTOMATED STORE OF THE FUTURE** in which computers receive customers' alphabetic computerized lists and robots assemble the order. Or, if customers still preferred to list by categories, the computer could perhaps translate their lists into bar codes, as electronic cash registers now turn bar codes into prices.

I've lingered over the shopping list because it illustrates beautifully how form and function relate. Written lists serve to organize and facilitate shopping. As shopping changes, the form and use of the list changes. In turn, the form of the lists can lead to changes in shopping and even, perhaps, in the organization of stores. Television and computer catalogs have already led to new forms of merchandizing, for example.

The tenor of relationships between the writer and reader of the shopping list is a powerful determiner of the list characteristics. My mother's lack of trust in the store clerk, my own concern about not getting cheated, modern shoppers' awareness of how stores encourage impulse buying, all strongly influence the shopping list genre. If the list reader is not also the writer, the list must be more explicit. The writer may write in large underscored print: DO NOT BUY ANYTHING THAT ISN'T ON THE LIST! If I did that, or committed any other shopping miscue, my mother would say, "Didn't you read the list?" She had great faith in the power of writing and reading.

The relationship of form and function is similar for all genres of language from the most formal to the least formal. Not long ago the *TV Guide* was primarily a list of programs for various channels, arranged by time and day, with brief blurbs for each program. Today's *TV Guide* provides a compact two-dimensional table showing all offerings at each time slot, but to stay within the limited space, it has reduced the amount of information for each listing. The guide may still offer a chronological listing, but only of the major channels, with special lists for sports programs and films and an additional alphabetic listing of all films shown during the week. Numerical codes are provided with each listing so it's easier for viewers to record programs on their VCR.

Again these changes illustrate not only how form changes to accommodate function and social custom, but also how user needs become constraints on the form. The alphabetic list of movies relates to the sheer number of choices cable subscribers have and the limited space available for descriptive information.

Presentation of and access to large amounts of information demand trade-offs. Smaller print in tables and lists is an option, but you can't read easily what you can't see clearly. Print too dense lacks aesthetic appeal and may disturb readers, so publishers have to provide white space and varied format. Varying the size of fonts may convey relative importance and create an attractive appearance, but they limit the amount of information provided.

Non-alphabetic features and languages

At the beginning of the first chapter I deliberately asked you to focus on yourselves as readers, rather than on the reading of letters and words, because I wanted to expose some erroneous beliefs about literacy. Reading is not first of all about letters or words, but about meaning. I want to reinforce that point now by highlighting how much non-alphabetic information is part of the written English language, and how non-alphabetic features also have their origin in function. A lot of published texts make rich use of the non-alphabetic aspects of our writing systems. And, of course, many people don't use alphabetic writing at all.

Fonts and design

In anticipation of these comments about fonts, I deliberately used a few **different fonts** in the previous section. Because fonts evoke culturally-based meaning responses in readers, they are an important non-alphabetic aspect of written language. Newspaper pages use fonts, type size, boldness, white space, line dividers and boxes, pictures, graphics and diagrams to organize, relate, separate and assign relative importance to the information being presented:

> The front page of the newspaper provides an intricate layout . . . The style books which specify typefaces and placements, rules and other conventions for front and editorial pages are often over two-hundred pages in length. The front page, itself, has typically between thirty and fifty modulations of typeface, size and style alone. (Storkerson, 1993, p.425)

All this design is not just intended to make the newspaper more attractive. It combines different symbol systems to represent the information more completely than alphabetic writing can by itself. It makes it easier for the reader to select news items and features and to comprehend more completely. Page design used to require a highly skilled, artistic specialist, but now computers handle the job.

Non-alphabetic writing systems

Modern society also uses writing systems that are not alphabetic at all. Here are two ways of writing the same thing:

17 + 33 = 50
Seventeen plus thirty-three equals fifty.

The first form uses numerals and symbols to represent ideas. The numerals 1, 2, 3, etc. stand for numbers; numbers are the ideas or concepts the numerals stand for. That makes the numerals ideographs. The second form uses the

English alphabet. Mathematical sentences are seldom written alphabetically, because ideographic writing has a number of advantages (another pun).

➤ The meaning of the ideographic sentence is independent of any oral language, so it can be read and understood by people who don't speak English. This form of representing mathematical relationships is almost universal in the modern world.

➤ The form of the writing can itself represent the number system (1 and 7 are themselves numerals), but when I write them together — 17 — I am representing the decimal system. Now the 1 has the value of 10 because of its place in the two-digit sequence.

➤ That makes it possible to symbolically manipulate mathematical concepts by manipulating the writing system.

$$\begin{array}{r} 17 \\ +33 \\ \hline 50 \end{array} \qquad \begin{array}{r} 50 \\ -33 \\ \hline 17 \end{array} \qquad \begin{array}{r} 17 \\ \times 4 \\ \hline 68 \end{array} \qquad ^{68}/_4 = 17$$

All of us have learned to add, subtract, multiply and divide by performing operations on the non-alphabetic written form. If we encounter the alphabetic form in a "problem" — *How much is fifty minus thirty-three?* — we often have to rewrite it in the non-alphabetic form to "solve" it.

Higher forms of mathematics are even more dependent on the use of ideographic representation. The compact formula $A=\Pi r^2$ translates into a mouthful: *The area of a circle is equal to the product of the ratio of the diameter to the circumference (a constant) times the square of the radius.*

Modern technology uses numerical coding for many things: machines translate electrical energy, heat, light and sound into numerals which are then stored or transmitted and subsequently translated back to the original or alternate outputs — light to sound, for example. My "multi-media" computer can represent musical sound with a visual scale and show a written score while it plays a song. Numerical coding is used to create compact discs, computers and imaging in electronics, and to control complex machine operations in industry. Science also uses complex formulas to represent and manipulate complex relationships.

Using non-alphabetic writing for math and science is not only compact and manipulable, it also has the value of making them independent of any one language and thus comprehensible internationally and interlingually. (I think I just made that word up.) Anyone who has a math or science background can construct coherent meaning from non-alphabetic writing. I once saw an economics dissertation in the field of money policies which was only 20 pages long, half of it formulas. I couldn't read them, but I'm sure they made sense to the student and her committee.

Icons and symbols

Icons and symbols have been around for a very long time. We still use some icons that various medieval guilds invented, such as the barber pole and the three balls for the pawn shop. The scale represents justice and the Caduceus is the physicians' symbol. Icons and symbols are highly effective at communicating meaning in many contexts in modern literate societies.

In the mid-1970s, the American Institute of Graphic Arts designed a set of symbols (see overpage) to be used in airports, train stations, etc. They had to be readable from a distance under varying light conditions. Alphabetic writing wouldn't work, since not all travelers read a single language. Some of the symbols are true icons, like the phone receiver; some are simply widely recognized symbols, like the red cross, here used as a first-aid sign.

The committee established consistency in design features (layout, size, colors) and conformity to a size-distance formula (how big it must be to be readable at the desired distance). Even so, they warned (p.180), "Experienced designers know that the same visual elements may function differently in different surroundings." It won't do to put a yellow sign on a yellow wall, for example.

How many of these symbols can you make sense of? Which one points to the lost and found? Do you think of umbrellas and gloves as commonly lost items? Do the question marks suggest to you that these are places to go for information? (Many places now use a large "I" instead.) Which of these symbols says "Do not enter"? Which one tells where shops are located? The elevator?

How many have become universal since their creation, or at least common enough for you to find them familiar? It takes more than an official body's blessing to make symbols and icons universally acceptable. Even those that are explicit icons with pictographs of an object (the cup, for example) have meaning only to those who have learned that this means "Beverages available." A symbol becomes a social convention only when there's a shared social meaning.

Icons and symbols used along freeways have to be read at rapid speeds. I saw this moose icon on a road in Sweden, inside a red triangle. Although I'd never seen this particular icon, I was familiar with similar ones that portray cattle, deer and other animals (I even saw a koala in Australia), so it had meaning at first sight: "Watch for moose crossing here."

Some businesses spend large sums of money on logos to ensure instant recognition of their company and its products in a wide range of circumstances. Fast food restaurants and many other commercial enterprises are using icons on cash register buttons for speed and ease of use.

Computers have introduced new icons to represent programs, processes and objects. Clicking a "mouse" cursor on them saves typing commands into the computer and even makes it possible for inexperienced computer users who don't know the commands to control the computer. Computers are also capable of sophisticated graphic and multimedia displays for communicating "virtual reality." Already there are primitive virtual reality programs that turn a graphic representation into a close approximation of the real experience. Whether they will be able to achieve all that's promised (up to and including virtual sex) has yet to be seen, heard and felt.

All of these forms of writing are superior to alphabetic writing *in certain situations for certain language functions.* Alphabetic writing is important, but it's only one of several systems modern literate societies use for written language communication.

Non-alphabetic languages

We tend to forget when we're discussing literacy that several modern cultures prefer to use a non-alphabetic writing system. By over-valuing alphabetic writing, we under-value the non-alphabetic writing used by millions of modern people: the Chinese, the Japanese and other societies with a long history of literacy.

There's a common misconception that the Chinese never knew about the alphabetic writing that was developed in the middle east and subsequently adapted to modern European languages. I call this "the Marco Polo fallacy." Western people think the Chinese didn't know about Europe because the Europeans didn't know about China. Actually, Marco Polo followed well-established caravan trails made by Chinese silk merchants. The fact is that the Chinese were well informed about alphabetic writing, tried it at several points in their history, and each time rejected it.

Most recently, the People's Republic tried to initiate a transition from Chinese ideographic writing to an alphabetic writing form using the Pin-yin alphabet, based on the Roman alphabet but adapted to represent the Chinese sound system. That plan was largely abandoned after the initial stage, which simplified some Chinese characters and shifted from right-to-left vertical to left-to-right horizontal writing.

There are lots of reasons for the Chinese decision to remain with a non-alphabetic system:

➤ Obviously, their written language works for them; it serves the functions they need it for.

➤ After many centuries of use, a huge literature exists, embedded in deeply rooted cultural tradition.

➤ Because the writing is ideographic, like our math system, it can be comprehended by people who speak a variety of dialects (which are really different languages).

➤ Writing with characters takes less space and uses less paper than alphabetic writing requires.

➤ Over centuries of use, the characteristics of their writing system have developed to become a good fit for the language.

Essentially the same reasons hold for the Japanese and Koreans, for example, both of which are based to some extent on the Chinese written forms. Korea has switched in this century to syllabic characters, but Chinese characters are also still in use.

What the successful, widepread use of non-alphabetic language teaches us is that *it is possible to make sense of print directly without relating the print to oral language.* And that's true even with alphabetic writing.

Summary

Language is a living, dynamic organism. All people and all peoples create language forms to meet their personal and social needs — we've done that throughout human history, and we'll keep doing it as long as our species exists. Because the form of the language we create depends on its function and genre, even those forms that serve routine purposes change and develop in response to specific human needs. This is true not only of oral and alphabetic written language, but of non-alphabetic features and languages as well.

We must guard against talking about literacy in terms of alphabetic writing only. Too much emphasis on the particular features of alphabetic writing may cause us to miss the more universal characteristics of writing systems as ways of expressing and communicating meaning. Then we drift into the misconception that writing is secondary to speech, that it represents speech rather than meaning.

Although there is a systematic relationship between oral language and written language, whether alphabetic or non-alphabetic, ultimately it's meaning, not speech, that print represents. One reason the importance of this print-meaning relationship hasn't been well enough understood in Western countries is the ethnocentric concentration on alphabetic writing only in North American and European scholarly writing.

4

*What
you think you
see is more important than
what your eyes
pick up.*

How proficient reading works

After exploring how the form of language relates to its function, we can start digging into how the reading and writing processes actually work. In this chapter I'm going to ask you to read some texts, examine what you do in the process, and then reflect on how reading works for you.

First this question: if researching literacy processes is so easily possible, why don't all readers fully and completely understand how reading and writing work? Ironically, we've become so good at making sense of written language that we find it hard to understand what we do as we read and write. The processes work so well that we have difficulty analyzing what we're doing. It's like trying to explain how you drive a car to someone who's trying to learn.

But there's something else that gets in the way of our understanding: a set of misconceptions about language. We continue to believe that certain things are true even though our own experiences with language repeatedly contradict those beliefs. In this chapter you'll demonstrate to yourself that some very widely held beliefs about reading are wrong.

For example, a lot of people believe that readers see each letter in each word and identify it in some way. In fact, now that I've said that, you probably are seeing each letter and each word separately. Because you've become consciously analytical, your reading supports the view that you see and process everything. What's happened, however, is that you've changed your focus, and by focussing on each letter and each word instead of on meaning, you've stopped using the reading process to make sense. When you start wondering whether you say each word to yourself as you see them, you find yourself saying them. And since you're literate, if you think about it when you hear someone speaking, you may also see in your mind the printed words that represent the words you're hearing. Try it as you listen to friends talk.

The following experiments might help to elucidate the reading process.

What you see ain't what you get!

DIRECTIONS:

Read the following paragraph through once and only once.

When you've finished, cover it.

Write down everything you remember reading.

Don't reread the paragraph until I tell you to.

You may want to reread the instructions before you read the paragraph. Remember, and this is important: read the story only once and then write down everything you remember reading.

The Boat in the Basement

A woman was building a boat in her
basement. When she had finished the
the boot, she discovered that it was
too big to go though the door. So he
had to take the boat a part to get
it out. She should of planned ahead.

Discussion

*We read with our brain,
not with our
eyes.*

Did you have any trouble understanding this story? In fact, you pretty well knew how it was going to turn out before you got to the end, didn't you? It's *predictable*: it's a familiar situation and the meaning is within your conceptual grasp since you know about boats, basements, doors and amateur builders. That's why you found yourself anticipating what would happen, leaping ahead to the meaning of the whole story.

Before we discuss your comprehension any further, take a careful look at your rewriting. Did you write in *cursive* or in printing (**manuscript**)? Remember, I told you to write down everything you remembered *reading*. If you wrote in cursive, as I expect most of you did, then your interpretation of "reading" doesn't include the form of the writing, since your rewriting doesn't look like what you read. This use of your own handwriting is not a trifling phenomenon, because it shows that you wrote *what you understood, not what you saw*. In reading, your brain treats the different forms of the print as equivalent, perceiving the printed form but producing a form preferred for writing. The form is more or less incidental to the reading process.

Now I know from experience that some of you were bothered by what seemed to be a typo or two. How many did you notice? Whoa! Don't look back at the original paragraph, not yet! And if you didn't notice anything wrong, don't worry either — you may turn out to be among the more proficient readers.

Did you spot *boot* where you expected to find *boat*? Did you reread at that point, even though you were instructed not to, to clear up the confusion? There's a body of research on eye-movement regressions in reading. There have even been machines created to teach readers not to regress; they wipe out the text immediately after it is read. But your regression here (or the temptation to make one) can't be a problem if it helped you to understand what you were reading. You reread because you needed to make sense of the story.

Some of you saw *boot* but wrote *boat* anyway. That's because you were predicting *boat* so strongly that you decided to reject the typo. Many of you will also have written *she* rather than *he* near the end of the story, because you knew that the story had no male character and the pronoun should refer to the woman. Again, the likelihood that you noticed this error is related to your strong prediction of meaning.

Boat and *boot* look alike and both are nouns. *He* and *she* also look alike and both are pronouns. Yet in spite of these commonalities, you likely spotted the errors because they violated your strong expectations with respect to meaning. Our brains focus on making sense in reading. That also helps to explain why you might not have noticed the other "errors" in this text.

A part should be *apart*. The two-word noun phrase, composed of the article *a* and the noun *part*, can't fit grammatically and doesn't make sense. You may have missed this because your expectation of what was coming in the text, based on the meaning you were constructing, was so strong that all you needed to see was some of what you expected, enough to confirm your prediction. Notice I'm talking about predictions, inferences and confirmations here, not accurate word identification. Your focus is not on recognizing words but on making sense of print. You are constructing meaning.

Now go ahead and reread the story, but don't be surprised or discouraged if you still miss the three other "errors" I planted. In a research study (Gollasch, 1980), most people couldn't find all six errors, even with unlimited time to search for them.

You probably thought you saw *through* in line four, but it actually says *though*. Did you write "through the door" when you rewrote the story? If so, you've provided more evidence that reading isn't seeing each letter, noting the sequence of letters, deciding what the word is (it's "name"), and then going on to the next word.

Reading isn't simply recognizing words in succession. Something propels you forward as you read, helps you to anticipate so well what's coming that you simply use *cues* from the print to move constantly toward meaning. Your brain is not a prisoner of the senses; it's in charge of the process! It sets up expectations and instructs your eyes to glide over the surface of the print, using that input to make sense of the text.

In this case, your brain was so confident that your eyes scanned the text several times without noticing that what you read as *through* is missing a letter and pronounced quite differently. Your brain has developed strategies to limit the amount of perceptual information it uses to just enough for making sense of the print and confirming its predictions. It knows that too much information from those "ough" words slows down meaning-making. You saw enough to confirm your expectation, and although *through* and *though* actually differ more than *a part/apart* and *boot/boat*, you didn't notice the error as readily because of the confidence you had in your prediction. You were so sure of what you had perceived that you rejected disconfirmation each time you reread. In reading, what you think you see is more important than what you actually see. Perception is a brain activity. It builds on sensory input — what your eyes pick up — by applying one or more schemas to make it sensible. Perception is what you *think* you see.

Now look at the last line of the story, where you'll find *should of* instead of *should've*. The latter is the contraction for *should have*. *Of* is a very common word with an unusual spelling for its usual pronunciation. (For an easy win, bet someone he or she can't accurately count the <f>s on a page of print. Almost everyone will miss some of those in *of*.) The <of> and <ve> both represent the same sound pattern, but they have very different grammatical functions; *of* doesn't make sense after *should*. Even so, it's a common spelling error. Graphically this error should have been the easiest to detect, since the visual difference is greatest. Again it's the strength of your prediction and your focus on meaning-making that kept you from perceiving it.

If you didn't notice some of these errors, you're not a poor reader but an efficient one: you concentrated on the sense and weren't distracted by errors. Efficient reading is getting to meaning with the least amount of effort.

I've saved the sixth error because it's both the most obvious and the hardest to detect. If you still don't know what it is, take the time now to reread until you find it or finally give up.

Are you back? If you still didn't find it, look at the end of line two and the beginning of line three, where *the* is repeated. A whole extra word! Why was it so hard to see if reading is a careful, successive recognition of words and letters? This should have been the easiest of the six errors to detect, since the double occurrence of *the* is all but impossible in English grammar. (One possibility would be: "You left *the the* out of that line.") It isn't that your eyes don't see both words, but that your brain rejects the likelihood. The eyes are tools of the brain. The brain tells them where to look and what to look for. It decides what to attend to and use from what the eye reports. The brain is completely in charge of all human information processing. So, when your eye sent the input for the repeated *the*, your brain's response was: "Don't get sloppy. I've got that information already!"

The human mind must be selective in reading. It must develop schemas and strategies for perceiving and making decisions quickly before all the available information has been processed. Life is constantly requiring us to make informed decisions using incomplete and ambiguous information, whether reading, playing a game, or just walking down the street. In reading, we're constantly using what we already know to make inferences, anticipate and predict what we don't know yet.

Expectation of form, structure and — most of all — meaning is what reading is all about. What we think we see is partly what we see but more what we expect to see. And what we expect to see has such a strong influence that, as long as we're making sense of the text, we overlook our own miscues and the writer's or printer's errors. On the other hand, those miscues that really interfere with making sense are not only detected but corrected, as in your reading of this little story.

Confirm for yourself that your experience here is not unique. Try this experiment on some of your friends. With minor differences, you'll see that their reactions are like yours. All readers use the same strategies to make sense of print.

For his doctoral dissertation, Fred Gollasch asked junior high and university students to read this same story. Half of each group was told to look for errors, the other half to read for meaning. Here are some of the findings:

➤ With limited exposure (enough time to read the paragraph one to three times), subjects found around one-third of the errors. Those told to look for errors found 37%, on average. Those looking for meaning found 28%.

➤ The junior high students as a group found 32%; the college students found 42%.

This shows that, while college students are more flexible than junior high students, and those who are looking for errors find more than those who aren't, the errors did not distract most readers from making sense of what they were reading.

After the first rewriting, Gollasch permitted his subjects to reread the story and take unlimited time to search for the remaining mistakes. Even then, junior high readers found only 59% and college students only 69%. And the six errors kept the same order of difficulty across both groups and conditions — all powerful evidence of what you experienced yourself, namely that reading is not recognizing words but making sense of print.

Now think about this: as you read the paragraph, you focussed primarily on its meaning and overlooked several errors. You overlooked them because you were being successful constructing meaning and you had strong expectations of what you were going to find in the text. Obviously, the same process governed your reading of the rest of the text as well — you weren't looking at every letter in the other words either. The fact that you read those words as expected isn't an indication of your concern for letter and word accuracy, but of your efficiency in using just enough information from what you were seeing to confirm what you predicted would be there.

In this little study you have seen that good reading is not a matter of careful attention to detail or concern for accuracy. Effective reading keeps the focus on making sense, and with that focus the other things assume proper importance.

Sense and nonsense

I've been talking, and will continue to talk throughout the book, about the importance of readers making sense of what they read. Together you and I have demonstrated that readers get to the meaning without attending to all the detail of the letters and the words. That doesn't imply, however, that readers are constructing meaning through some kind of unknowable mystic process. Language is at work when we read and it is through transacting with language that we construct meaning. Yet the meaning is never *in* the language. Readers and writers must bring meaning *to* language so they can construct meaning *from* language. Language simply has meaning potential. Writers create texts with meaning potential that reflects the meaning in their heads, and readers bring sufficient meaning to those texts to make sense of them.

In the next experiment we're going to try to make sense of a text deliberately devoid of meaning. We want to discover what it is in language that you, as a reader, use to make sense of a text. Although the story is a real one, every content word has been removed and replaced by a nonsense word with English-like pronunciation and spelling. Since English grammar makes strong use of sentence patterns, however, it's possible to assign grammatical functions to the nonsense words and thus sustain the meaning potential. The function words — the words that tie the text together and set up the grammatical patterns — have been retained, but they don't have much in the way of definable meanings themselves. Also in place are the inflections, the word endings that English grammar uses to mark words for grammatical functions, nouns and verbs primarily.

DIRECTIONS:

Read the story all the way through.

Answer the questions that follow, using the language of the story.

A Mardsan Giberter for Farfie

Glis was very fraper. She had denarpen Farfie's mardsan. She didn't talp a giberter for him. So she conlanted to plimp a mardsan binky for him. She had just sparved the binky when he jibbled in the gorger.

"Clorsty mardsan!" she boffed.

"That's a crouistish mardsan binky," boffed Farfie, "but my mardsan is on Stansan. Agsan is Kelsan."

"In that ruspen," boffed Glis, "I won't whank you your giberter until Stansan.

1. Why was Glis fraper?
2. What did Glis plimp?
3. Who jibbled in the gorger when Glis sparved the binky?
4. What did Farfie bof about the mardsan binky?
5. Why didn't Glis whank Farfie his giberter?

This nonsense is so much like English that you have the feeling that it ought to make sense to you. The problem is that you are culturally disadvantaged. You've had little experience with being *fraper*. You don't know what happens to a *mardsan* when it is *denarpen*, or the preferred way to *plimp* a *mardsan binky*. And certainly if you don't know what makes a *mardsan binky* a *crouistish* one, it will be difficult to make sense of this sentence and story.

On the whole, the difference between sense and nonsense in any language is the extent of a particular reader's related experience and his or her familiarity with the terms and concepts. We are all functionally illiterate to some extent. I get a lawyer to read contracts for me, and I hereby admit to perjury! I lie when it says above my signature: "I have read and understood all of the above." And don't ask me to make sense of knitting instructions.

Let's see, first, how well you were able to do on the questions.

➤ *Why was Glis fraper?* That's easy: *She had denarpen Farfie's mardsan.*

➤ The second — *What did Glis plimp?* — isn't much more difficult. *She plimped a mardsan binky for Farfie.*

➤ The third is easy too: *Who jibbled in the gorger?* Farfie did, of course.

➤ And no doubt you knew that what *Farfie boffed* was: *"That's a crouistish mardsan binky."*

➤ Question 5 is what basals call an "inference" question. Give yourself credit if you answered something like: "She didn't talp a giberter for Farfie." Of course, you may have been fooled and answered: "She didn't whank Farfie his Giberter because his mardsan isn't until Stansan." If you thought that, then you missed the humor of the whole story. Oh well, some people have difficulty recognizing humor in literature.

Now let's go back to the first sentence of the story. Even with the nonsense words, you had little problem dealing with this as an English sentence. You know that *Glis* is the subject, probably a proper noun. You know that *fraper* is an adjective that says something about *Glis*. This sort of sentence pattern is common in English: a subject noun followed by a form of "be" and an adjective: *John is handsome. The girl was hungry. The car will be expensive.*

Whatever *fraper* means, you know it relates to the noun *Glis*. And since the next sentence starts with the pronoun *she*, you infer that *Glis* is female. That's what you would do if you were reading real words, too: infer the referent of a pronoun using the cohesion and grammar of the text.

You also know which word in the second sentence is the verb. It's *denarpen*. In this subject-verb-object sentence, the subject is *she*, the object is *Farfie's mardsan* and the verb is *denarpen*. You know because of:

➤ its position between the subject and object;

➤ the function word *had*, which precedes it;

➤ the -*en* ending.

In fact, you've inferred a past perfect transitive verb, whether you were aware you knew all that or not. You could even confidently guess what some of the other forms of this verb must be: *I denarp, he/she denarps, I am denarping, I denarped, I will denarp.* See how well you know and use English grammar? You could do similar things with the verb *talp* in the next sentence: *talp, talps, talped, talping.*

You also use grammar to identify nouns. *Giberter* is a noun: it follows *a*. You know what its plural must be: *giberters*, spelled with an <s> but pronounced /z/. How can you be so sure of how to pronounce this plural form but not the rest of the word? Simple: you're using your knowledge of English orthography and its relationship to English phonology (the sound system). After words ending in the /r/ sound you always use the /z/ form. But the rules are a bit less consistent for the <g>. Before <i> is it soft as in "gin" or hard as in "give"? Does the stress go on the first or second syllable: "gí-ber-ter" or "gi-bér-ter"? You can be sure of the grammar but not the pronunciation of the nonsense words. As a proficient reader, you could produce a pronunciation for every one of them. Yours might not agree with anybody else's, however, and there's no way of settling on a single "correct" pronunciation because the phonics of various English dialects is too complex.

Mardsan is an interesting word because it appears as a noun in some places: *Farfie's mardsan*, and as a noun modifier in others: *mardsan binky*. English words can change their syntactic function, but you know the function by the pattern in which you find it. We use the *garden* hose in the *garden* when we're *gardening*.

In this story, the patterns of English grammar, which give the text system, form and shape, are constantly leading you toward meaning. If you knew what *plimp* meant, or *mardsan*, or *binky*, you could make sense of the story. Just one tiny bit of meaning would be all you'd need to understand the rest — for instance, what kind of *mardsan* is a *clorsty* one and why does it rate an exclamation mark?

What you've shown yourself is that readers use language patterns to get to meaning. You have everything you need to get to meaning in this nonsense story, but you can't quite get there because you don't bring enough meaning to the reading. You're sensing the interrelationships of the ideas in this story from the grammatical patterns, but you don't have enough experience with *mardsans*, *Agsans*, *Kelsans* and *Stansans*. Wait a minute! Did I see a pattern there? *On Stansan*? *Until Stansan*? Why the capitals?

Something like this happens to all readers, no matter how proficient, when they try to read a text containing concepts, ideas and terminology which are over their heads, when they lack the background to understand the content. They can only play with it as nonsense. If they read it aloud, they can produce reasonably good intonations and pronunciations, so it sounds like language that makes sense to them. Kids do it all the time in school. Too often students in upper elementary and secondary grades have given up on making sense of what they're asked to read. They make it sound pretty good, and they do as well answering comprehension questions as you did with the nonsense questions following this story. When asked: "What are the principal features of Antarctica?," kids learn to go back through the book looking for a sentence that starts: *The principal features of Antarctica are...* and copy what follows. You don't have to know any more about a "principal feature" than you do about a "mardsan binky" to get the answer right. Ironically, if you do bring a bit of prior knowledge to such a question, you may not match the textbook well enough and your answer will be marked wrong.

The point is that it's possible to manipulate meaningful language as if it were nonsense. That says a lot about the need for our students to be reading materials relevant to their experiences. Unfamiliar language used to discuss unfamiliar concepts unrelated to the reader's experience is nonsense to the reader.

An unexpected thing began to happen when I started using this nonsense story with adult audiences. Almost every time, one or more people in the audience could reconstruct the original meaningful story, yet invariably they had no idea how they did it. I think I know what happens. Patterns like the one I hinted at suggest enough about the time (or other) relationships for readers to build on and so construct a meaning very close to the original. Once they can give meanings to even a few of the nonsense words it becomes easier to make sense of the rest. Did you get the story's meaning? (Here's one more clue: *Happy birthday!*)

This experiment (see also chapter six) has shown us that readers use three kinds of information to make sense of what they read:

➤ Graphophonic
You used your knowledge of English orthography, spelling and punctuation to produce an oral reading of the nonsense story. You also used your knowledge of the phonology, or sound system, and of how orthography and phonology relate to each other: that's phonics. You could easily produce possible English pronunciations, although there's no way to tell what the conventional pronunciation would be in any particular dialect of English (in New England I'd expect to hear "mahdsan"). It's obvious, however, that being able to say nonsense doesn't make it sensible.

➤ Grammatical (syntactic)
You were able to assign acceptable English grammar to the sentences in the story and even knew what part of speech (grammatical function) each nonsense word had. That told you a lot about what's happening in the story, but without real meaning. Halliday (1975) refers to this connection between grammar and wording (lexicon) in the term "lexico-grammar."

➤ Semantic (meaning)
The third kind of information is meaning and you just showed yourself that you must bring meaning to the text to get meaning from it.

We use all three kinds of information to make sense of what we read. And the more meaning we bring to the reading, the less information from the other systems we need in order to make sense of it. Fortunately, we seldom meet a text with as many unfamiliar words as this nonsense text has — usually only one or two, although at times we may find a familiar word used in an unfamiliar context with an unfamiliar meaning. And we get additional meaning, as well, from the situational and cultural context the text occurs in.

Getting the word

Let's do a third experiment to see how we build up our reading vocabularies as we encounter unfamiliar words in context. In this experiment we'll ask this question: *How does a word acquire meaning for a particular reader?*

First, consider this: a concept or idea and the way of expressing that concept or idea in language are two different, though related, things. For example,

➤ we may have the concept but be unfamiliar with particular wording to express it;

➤ we may know the word but be unfamiliar with a particular use of it;

➤ or we may have neither the concept nor the wording.

Once I observed a fifth-grade teacher "introducing the new words" before the class tackled reading a story. The teacher asked for a definition of "cowardice." After several attempts by the students were rejected, one student checked the book's glossary and won praise from the teacher for offering: "showing fear in the face of danger." The teacher seemed to feel that if the student could state the book definition he understood the word. But I had heard several kids mumbling "chicken" under their breath. They had the concept but not the term.

DIRECTIONS:
Read one sentence at a time, keeping the rest covered.
Decide what you think "pali" means each time you pause.
Notice how your meaning changes as you add more context.

The Pali

Several years ago I saw a pali for the first time. Pali is a Hawaiian word, but everyone in the island state uses it. The first pali I saw was very high. It was a pali near Honolulu which has great historical significance. People in Honolulu call it, simply, "the Pali." On this pali, the first King Kamehameha trapped the army of Oahu and drove his enemies off the Pali to their deaths.

The wind blows so strongly up the face of the Pali that you can hardly approach the edge. A local tale is that one day a despondent lover jumped off the Pali and the wind held him up against the face of the Pali until the firemen could come and rescue him.

As you progressed through this story, you came to know more and more about the word and the concept *pali*, and your meaning got closer and closer to the conventional Hawaiian meaning. Your meaning may have moved from thing to place, to type of place, to a specific example, to more and more sense of what makes a pali a pali and what is special about "the Pali" near Honolulu. The point is, your understanding of the word and concept built as you were using them in this authentic literacy event.

If you live in an area with similar formations, you probably have the concept and found it easy to get the meaning and equate the meaning to one or more terms you use. If you live in a flat place, you'll have little experience to relate to this text and it may have taken you longer to build a meaning — perhaps you still hadn't by the end of the reading.

To make the whole process more difficult, the meaning you assign to fit this text may not fit the next text you see it in. To build our vocabulary, we need successive experiences with words and phrases encountered in authentic texts. Of course, if you live in Hawaii or have been there and visited the Pali or other palis, you were familiar with the concept and the term before you read the text. We can build a meaning through reading, but that's not the same as leaning into the howling wind as you walk toward the edge of the Pali.

The drive for meaning

Readers construct their own meaning as they read.

So far I've violated my own belief that reading should be studied by looking at real readers reading real texts, not contrived experimental research texts that control the complex variables in language. We've looked at a text sprinkled with deliberate errors, a text filled with nonsense words, and a real-language text set up to show you how you learn new vocabulary. At least my experimental texts are based solidly on an understanding of what makes a text a text, but now we need a really real text, with no tricks.

In this experiment we'll use the beginning of a real adult short story. Reflecting on your reading of it will help you discover how you use the reading process to make sense of an authentic text.

DIRECTIONS:
Have a blank piece of paper and a pencil ready.
Read the paragraph through *just one time*.
Cover the book and write down everything you remember reading, without looking back.
Compare what you read with what you wrote.

Poison

It must have been around midnight when I drove home, and as I approached the gates of the bungalow I
switched off the head lamps of the car
so the beam wouldn't swing in through
the window of the side bedroom and
wake Harry Pope.

I won't repeat my earlier comments about the visual difference between the printed fonts and your handwriting (computer, typewriter). Let me ask these questions instead: How many sentences were there in the story as you rewrote it from memory? How many did the author use? Does it surprise you that the author used only a single sentence for these beginning lines of the story?

This is the introductory paragraph of a short story by Raold Dahl, who apparently felt it useful to use a single sentence to build background and suspense in the mind of the reader. If you used more than one sentence, where did you separate them? Are they equivalent to the clauses in the original paragraph? How much of the original paragraph did you leave out altogether? How many elements did you combine? Does your paragraph make sense or were you able to remember only bits and pieces? Did you get the gist of the paragraph even though you rewrote it considerably?

Now let's consider how Dahl crafted his opening sequence, assuming that this successful professional author did what he did quite deliberately.

First, why this one-word title, "Poison"? Might poison be a murder weapon in a mystery? Why does he start talking about time and why is he not precise? He could have said, "It was midnight" or even "The dashboard clock said 11:58." Why is the story in the first person? Is the "I" a man or a woman? Is the driver alone? Where are the gates of this bungalow and how can a car approach them? What is the driver's relationship to Harry Pope and why would he/she turn off the lights to avoid waking him? Is the driver being considerate or nefarious? Why is Harry's full name used?

Literature teachers have frequently assumed that reader comprehension means getting the precise meanings the author intended. But Dahl seems to be deliberately ambiguous here, teasing his readers into making inferences and predictions they'll be anxious to test by reading further. And Dahl is known for surprising his readers at the end of his stories.

What will happen next? Predictions will depend on the meaning each reader is constructing. Perhaps it's late. The driver is coming home and doesn't want to wake Harry Pope. So he/she quietly enters the bungalow and goes to bed. A possibility? No way! That's a logical next sequence, we know, but it would end our suspense and be an invitation to stop reading. Something far less likely is going to happen next. Dahl wants to surprise us, to keep us reading.

Look now at his use of grammar. I count six clauses in this one sentence.

It must have been around midnight
when I drove home **and**
as I approached the gates of the bungalow
I switched off the head lamps of the car
so the beam wouldn't
swing in through the window of the side bedroom **and**
wake Harry Pope.

Notice that the last two clauses share a common portion: *so the beam wouldn't* applies to both. The single "n't" negates both verbs, *swing* and *wake*. I marked the function words that tie these clauses together. Halliday and Hasan (1976) call the omissions of common elements and the use of conjunctions and other function words part of the *cohesion system* of the text, because they make it hang together. This opening has other cohesion devices as well. Notice that although the verbs *drove* and *approached* are used to indicate movement, it isn't until the word *car* appears that we can confirm our inference that the movement is by means of a car. The chain of related terms also builds cohesion.

Look at your own rewriting and see how much of what Dahl made implicit is explicit in your text and vice-versa. Are the clauses all there? Is your text equally cohesive?

At the end of the first line in the paragraph there is an unusual construction: *and as*. Most people who read this leave the *and* out in writing, reorganizing this portion of the paragraph into two separate sentences. To explain what's going on here I have to give you a small grammar lesson.

And is a conjunction that joins two language elements that have the same function: two verbs, *run and play*; two nouns, *Jack and Jill*; two adjectives, *red and blue*; two adverbs, *happily and easily*. It can join two clauses as well, but they must be equal, not dependent on each other. That's what *and* is doing in this paragraph. The problem is that the first independent clause (*It must have been around midnight*) is separated from *and* by a dependent clause (*when I drove home*). The second independent clause (*I switched off the head lamps of the car*) is separated from *and* by another dependent clause (*as I approached the gates of the bungalow*). On top of that, *as* has the function of making the clause it introduces dependent on an independent clause that follows it rather than precedes it.

And and *as* may be small function words, but they play important roles in helping readers make sense of this long opening sentence, by laying out the complex relationships between the clauses. (If Dahl had written this sentence in the tenth grade, would his teacher have written "run-on sentence" in the margin?) Actually, the *and* here is not really necessary. Take it out and you're left with two fine sentences. So why did the author put it in? I think he wants to propel us, his readers, into the story and keep us from pausing until we're caught up in it.

The purpose of paying attention to the ways you and Dahl put the clauses together isn't really to provide a grammar lesson, but to show that you had to cope with the grammatical structures to make sense of the text. You might have lost the meaning completely, although you understood each word. You had to deal with the grammatical sentence patterns (syntax) in order to understand the paragraph and rewrite what you understood. You may have produced more sentences, or different dependencies and clause combinations, of course, or you may actually have lost the relationships and misunderstood. The latter is the more serious matter.

Dahl wrote a complex text designed to be comprehensible to you as a member of his intended audience. But he didn't want it to be so comprehensible that you could know exactly what was on his mind at that point. He accomplished quite a lot in a few lines: gave us some sense of time and place; introduced two characters and made us wonder about their relationship; piqued our curiosity about what will happen next.

Now let's consider his choice of words. Did you substitute any words for his in your rewriting? For example, did you use *about* or *nearly* for *around*? Did you read *head lamps* but write *headlights* because that's what you expected on the basis of your experience? Is the name still *Harry Pope* or did you perhaps change it to *Henry* or *Mary*? Did the *bungalow* become a *cottage, cabin* or *house*?

Take another look at the word *bungalow*. Is there anything that bothers you about this bungalow of Dahl's? In Toronto, an audience told me that a bungalow always has one floor and three bedrooms. But it was the gates that bothered them more: they seem to suggest a substantial, closed-off driveway, more appropriate for an estate than a small home. Some suggested that the bungalow might be a gatehouse for a larger house farther back. The question is, how does your pre-existing concept of "bungalow" influence your ability to read and get a sense of the bungalow in this story? I know that many people omit references to the gates when rewriting this paragraph.

If you included *bungalow* correctly in your writing, does that prove you had a clear understanding of what it means here? If you left it out or substituted another word, does that mean you didn't get any sense of it? The answer is no in both cases. Accuracy doesn't mean the concept is fully understood and inaccuracy doesn't mean it isn't. After reading the whole story several hundred times, I thought I had a pretty complete understanding of the word used in this context. I knew it was an Indian word, and in India it denotes a much larger house than a North American bungalow. Later we find out that this one has a veranda with steps leading up to it. But it was only when a graduate student from India told me that in the period of this story bungalows were the substantial homes of British colonial officials that I realized the full significance of this bungalow for the plot of the story.

So what have we learned about reading from this authentic text experiment? Three things stand out:

➤ Readers must focus on meaning; attempting to make sense of the text is what drives the whole process.

➤ Readers clearly use language structures — the system or grammar of the language — to get to the meaning, by unraveling the clauses and their relationships. This is true of all authentic, cohesive texts. Without the system, the symbols can't represent meaning.

➤ Accuracy is a weak and unreliable indication of comprehension. In fact, too much concern for accuracy can get in the way of comprehension.

What you did during this final experiment was use three kinds of information — semantic (meaning), lexico-grammatical (the syntax and wording), and graphophonic (the letter patterns and their relationship to the sound patterns) — to read the author's text and construct your personal reader text. If both the author (the writer) and you (the reader) were successful, you comprehended. But remember — and this is important — there can never be total agreement between reader and writer about the meaning of the text.

Summary

In these experiments you studied your own reading process. You discovered how you achieve *effectiveness* (by successfully constructing meaning) while also being *efficient* (getting to meaning with the least amount of time, energy and visual input). You saw that reading is a far more efficient process than successively recognizing letters and words could ever be. And you discovered how active your mind is in making sense of print.

But you are a proficient adult reader. Is the same true for developing readers? We'll deal with that question in the next chapter.

5

*Miscues
show as many
reading strengths as they
do weaknesses and
problems.*

How developing reading works

In the preceding chapter you looked at yourselves as readers and got a sense of how proficient adults make sense of print. In this chapter we'll let kids show us how they develop reading proficiency and control of the reading process.

What I know about reading I learned from kids of all ages and proficiencies by asking them to read real, whole texts they hadn't seen before. I studied their miscues and built from that research the model and theory of written language that this book presents. You can do the same by observing it happening in these examples.

Miscues are points in oral reading where the *observed response* (OR) doesn't match the *expected response* (ER). Miscues provide windows on the reading process, because they show the reader attempting to make sense of the text. They reveal as much about the reader's strengths as they do about weaknesses.

Here are the marks I've used to note the miscues in the following children's readings:

➤ Omissions are enclosed in ( ) ; insertions appear above ∧ ; substitutions are printed above the words they replace.

➤ *(c)* indicates a correction, a *(uc)* an unsuccessful attempt at a correction; a line connects either with the point at which the correction begins.

➤ *(rs)* indicates a running start or a repetition that changes intonation without changing the wording.

➤ *($)* marks non-words.

High school students

We'll start with a group of high school students of varying proficiency, reading aloud the first paragraph of "Poison," the same paragraph you read. In each case they continued to read the whole story.

1.   It must have been around mid-

night when I drove home, and as I ap-

proached the gates of the bungalow I

(c) lights

switched off the head \lamps of the car

on

so the beam wouldn't swing in through

the window of the side bedroom and

wake Harry Pope.

2.   It must have been around mid-

(c)

night when I drove home, \and (as) I ap-

proached the gates of the bungalow I

(c) lights

switched off the head \lamps of the car

so the beam wouldn't swing in through

the window of the side bedroom and

wake Harry Pope.

3.   It must have been around mid-

.   *As*

night when I drove home, (and) as I ap-

proached the gates of the bungalow I

(c) lights

switched off the head \lamps of the car

so the beam wouldn't swing (in) through

You'll notice that these readers do some of the same things in their oral reading as you did in your written retelling. Look, for example, at the "and as" sequence. Reader 2 reads rapidly and confidently until she reaches that point. She omits "as," but it takes her four repetitions of "and" before she finally realizes it. She finally corrects and then switches to a slower pace with exaggerated emphasis on each word. Reader 3 omits "and," separating the two independent/dependent clause combinations into two independent sentences. Reader 5 omits "as" but adjusts for that by inserting "and" before "I switched," producing three independent clauses. All three solutions work.

All five of these readers show some activity around "head lamps." Four of them read "lights," but two correct. Reader 2 reads "lamps" first, changes to "lights" and then goes back to "lamps." Reader 5 leaves "lights" uncorrected. Reader 4 repeats "the head" before saying "lamps." They all show the power of expectation. Just as you did in "The Boat in the Basement," these readers make strong predictions based on the meaning and language the window of the side bedroom (and)

(c) where　　　　　*was-*
\\wake Harry Pope._____

4.　　　　　It must have been around midnight when I drove home, and as I ap-

　　　　　　　　　　　(c) 1.bung- 2.bung-
proached the gates of the \\bungalow I

　　　　(rs)
switched off \\the head lamps of the car

(rs)　　　　　　*(rs)*
　\\so the beam \\wouldn't swing (in) through
the window of the side bedroom and
wake Harry Pope.

5.　　　　　It must have been around midnight when I drove home, and (as) I ap-

　　　　　　　　　($)bugalog　　*and*
approached the gates of (the) bungalow ∧ I

　　　　　　lights
switched off the head lamps of the car

　　　　　　　(c)
so the beam wouldn't swing \\(in) through

　　　at　　　　　　*of the*
the window of the side ∧ bedroom and

　　　Henry
wake Harry Pope.

---

they bring to the story. Why "head lights" for "head lamps"? The latter is obviously a more familiar term, so they anticipate it. Some don't even correct. If it makes sense and matches their prediction, why correct? Their expectations are so strong that they're not aware they make the miscue.

Some stumble over "bungalow." Your own experience suggests we can't be sure that those who miscued didn't get any meaning here. Nor can we be sure that those who didn't miscue know what a bungalow is in this story.

"Swing in through" produced miscues for all but reader 2. Reader 1 reads "swing on through." Readers 3, 4 and 5 all omit "in," but only reader 5 corrects it. Each of these patterns produces a meaningful text, however: "swing through," "swing on through" and "swing in through" all fit the grammatical text with little or no meaning change.

Reader 5 produces a string of interesting miscues on the last two lines. Instead of "the window of the side bedroom," he moves to "the window at the side of the bedroom." His miscues change the syntax and meaning in minor ways but still fit and make sense. This same reader substitutes "Henry" for "Harry." He does that for most of the story. I suspect he knows a Henry but no Harry. And notice how much "Harry" and "Henry" look and sound alike. In England, a reader of his age might know that Harry is sometimes a nickname for Henry.

Reader 3 makes a miscue that doesn't quite work but that still shows the power of prediction. Remember I commented earlier about the complexity of clause structure. This reader omits the "and" that joins the two verbs "swing" and "wake," ending up with: "So the beam wouldn't swing through the window of the side bedroom where Harry Pope was . . ." You can tell that he had predicted "sleeping." But it isn't there, so he corrects back to "wake Harry Pope."

In your own experiment, you read the whole of the paragraph first and then produced a written representation, but oral readers go from print to meaning *while* producing an oral representation of that meaning. Although these students varied in proficiency, they all read the story with reasonable comprehension and relatively high-quality miscues — that is, with miscues that didn't cause much loss of meaning. We recognized their comprehension not only from analyzing their miscues but also from the oral retellings they did after their reading. I expect your conclusion, like mine, is that these students' oral reading is just as much a constructive process as your silent reading and subsequent retelling.

A nine-year-old

Let's look now at younger readers and how they use the reading process to construct their own texts and meaning. First we'll look at the miscues of Angela, an African-American from rural Mississippi, as she reads *The Little Brown Hen*, a trade book with a rural South setting and African-American characters. I'll display her text in single paragraphs, marking her miscues. We'll be looking at:

➤ how her miscues indicate her reading process; and

➤ how her rural African-American dialect and cultural experience show in her reading.

In miscue analysis, readers are usually asked to read aloud whole stories they haven't seen or read before. They aren't assisted. If they ask questions or ask for help, the researcher reminds them that they're on their own and encourages them to solve the problem themselves.

    Mr.   *his*

Mrs. Johnson opened the screen door, smoothing her blue apron. "How are you, Willie," she asked.

Here Angela substitutes "Mr." for "Mrs." and "his" for "the." That's not surprising if you consider that Willie has been talking to Mr. Johnson just before Mrs. Johnson appears for the first time. Young readers often miscue on Mr., Mrs. and Miss. But note here that having made "Mrs." into "Mr.," it follows that "the" screen door is "his" screen door. Prediction follows prediction for Angela, except that she doesn't correct, overtly anyway, when she gets to "her" and "she."

I am

Willie stood on one leg. "I'm fine," he said.

　　　(rs)　　　　　*(c)*　　*ma-made*

"I came \\<u>by</u> to see if you \\<u>had</u> ∧ any ducks hatched

(c)

\\<u>(out)</u> this year. Maw's birthday is tomorrow. She

wants a pair of ducks for her strawberry patch.

I'll　　　　　*(rs)*

I'd like to get \\<u>two</u> for her present."

Angela shifts from "I'm" to "I am," which is more common in her dialect. Throughout the reading she repeats words and phrases. She seems to change her mind about the syntactic structure she predicts, and usually her intonation changes to show that she has changed her mind. Here she repeats "by." Her first intonation makes it a preposition; her second makes it part of the verb "came by." She does the same kind of thing with "two," making it sound like the preposition "to." She seems to expect a noun to follow "two" and when it doesn't, she repeats and changes the intonation.

She also omits "out" after "hatched," then corrects her omission. (Words like "by" and "out" after verbs are verb particles. They're not prepositions but form new verbs different in meaning from the verbs they follow.) Angela predicts "made" after "had" in line three, then corrects, apparently deciding that what follows can't fit. Her last miscue in this paragraph is "I'll" for "I'd." These words look similar and they have the same function in the sentence, although there's a slight change in meaning: "I will like" instead of "I would like."

　　　　　well (rs)　　　　　　　*(uc)*

"There's nothing as good \\<u>as</u> a duck to keep \\<u>the</u>

　　　mugs　　　*the*　　　　　*Miss*

<u>weeds (and bugs)</u> out of a strawberry patch," Mrs.

Johnson said, "but I've not a single little duck.

(uc) I am really (c)　.　　(c) I have

\\<u>I'm real sorry,</u> \\∧<u>Willie</u>→. \\<u>I've</u> only my big white

pair. I thought my duck would lay this summer

but I haven't seen a sign of an egg."

Early in the first sentence, Angela substitutes "well" for "good" and makes a running start at "as." The former is an example of a substitution that fits the meaning and the syntax but has no resemblance to the text word, either as it looks or as it sounds. "Well" and "good" are synonyms in some contexts, but "well" is used as an adverb and "good" as an adjective. Children commonly use "good" as an adverb, however ("he did good"), and perhaps Angela has been corrected on that and thinks "well" the preferred form in all situations. The repetition on "as" may relate to Angela's recognizing the "as...as" pattern.

Her next miscue is complex. Originally she omits "and bugs," so she has "the weeds out of a strawberry patch." Then she corrects to read "the weeds and mugs out of a strawberry patch," producing a minor loss of meaning, perhaps due to a misarticulation (/m/ and /b/ are both labials — sounds made with the lips). Then she says "the" for "a." Since there has already been mention of "her strawberry patch," Angela treats it as definite, not any patch but a specific one already mentioned.

The next complex miscue suggests that Angela senses written language should be more formal than oral. The author has Mrs. Johnson saying "I'm real sorry," using the adjective "real" where the adverbial "really" would be more standard. No doubt she wanted the direct quote to sound more folksy. Although in her dialect Angela would probably herself use "real sorry," she reads this as "I am really sorry," again substituting for "I'm." That confirms our hunch that she did something similar with her "well/good" substitution. This time Angela corrects "really" to "real" but stays with "I am." This correction shows that she's closely monitoring her own predictions but, since it's for accuracy rather than meaning, it shows some inefficiency on her part.

She reads "Willie" as if it's the subject of a new sentence, omitting the period, but she immediately corrects, repeating and changing intonation to a sentence end. "I have" for "I've" again shows her more formal expectations of language in reading. Her correction is unnecessary, however, since meaning isn't disrupted.

kept	*The miscues in this*
"I keep wondering about my hen," Willie said.	*sequence show Angela's*
thought	*preoccupation with*
"I say it's no use wondering," Mr. Johnson said.	*meaning. Every miscue is*
	sensible. In two of them
food	*she stays close to the*
"Your hen's gone for good. No use worrying.	*orthography, substituting*
Just a waste of worry."	*"kept" for "keep" and*
	"food" for "good." This last

is one of my favorites of her miscues: hens are certainly used for food in her experience. Her substitution of "thought" for "say" involves both a shift in the verb and a change in tense, matching the shift from "keep" to "kept." Both tenses are acceptable in the story.

Her substitution of "thought" for "say" may be influenced by the author's use of "wondering." It shows that she's constructing her own text and its meaning. Both uses of "said" here involve direct speech, but the "say" doesn't; here it's an idiom meaning "my opinion is." That may also have influenced her substitution.

"Food" looks like "good" (although it doesn't rhyme with it), but here the idiom "for good" means permanently and has nothing to do with the meaning of "good."

"For" now takes on its purpose function and Angela has made "food" the purpose — quite logical for a farm child. Because her intonation is appropriate, we can infer that she hasn't simply mistaken "good" for "food." She doesn't correct because her prediction is not only meaningful to her, it also makes sense in the story.

Sceptical readers may be thinking, "How can he know what's going on in her mind?" I can't know for certain, of course, but there's nothing haphazard or random about Angela's miscues. It's easy to see her using all the cue systems of the language: graphophonic, syntactic and semantic, just as we demonstrated, in the previous chapter, that you do. This rural nine-year-old shows the language competence necessary to make sense of a meaningful text.

She also brings her knowledge of her world to her reading. In the process of reading an unfamiliar text, she constructs her own text and meaning, using her reading strategies and improving them in the process of using them. As she does so, she becomes more familiar with words, phrases and text styles. She learns to read by reading, and her miscues show this learning in progress. They also show her trying to make sense of the text — and largely succeeding.

A Samoan student

Next we look at a second-grade reader who is also a second-language speaker of English. We asked Fia, a Samoan child living in Honolulu, to read "Ah See and the Spooky House," a story set in Hawaii. Her miscues not only provide insights into her use of the reading process but also confirm sufficient control of English to comprehend what she is reading.

(rs) Ke-o-ki wen'
It was a sunny \day in Hawaii. Keoki ran
  bush   pas'
down the path from his house, past the
  base
taro patch to Antone's house.

Fia repeats "day," changing the intonation, perhaps to make it fit with "in Hawaii" or perhaps already aware that "Keoki" looks unfamiliar. In a sense she sounds out Keoki, but her final pronunciation — "kay-aw-key" — is definitely more Polynesian than English. (Keoki is the Hawaiian version of George. Samoan is closely related to Hawaiian. In both languages every vowel is a separate syllable.)

She substitutes "wen'" ("went") for "ran," which fits the meaning and grammar. "Bush" (for "path") and "base" (for "patch") are also real English nouns. In the islands, "bush" has the mainland meaning of "field" or "country," and she lives in an area of Honolulu were there are naval and air bases.

($)Antoe

"Antone!" he cried. "You know the house at the top of the Pali trail?"

($)Antoe   *($)duh*

Antone rubbed his ear. "You mean the

($)emplete   *($)axt*

empty one?" he asked.

($)emplete

"Yes, the empty one," said Keoki.

Fia reads "Antone" without a final /n/ sound, but with appropriate intonation for a proper noun and she is consistent through the story. It's rarely important to pronounce story names exactly right; most of us just say "Mr. R" if we can't pronounce Raskolnikov in reading a Russian novel. Twice she produces a non-word, "emplete," for "empty," perhaps an indication of her developing control of English. Has she made her own word using the ending of "complete"? Inventing possible words is common among kids, upwardly mobile adults and second-language learners. (In adults we call them malapropisms.)

The "duh" for "the" and "axt" for "asked" are examples of how the phonology of her island dialect influences the way she pronounces certain words. They aren't examples of Samoan influence, but of the English dialect used in her community.

(c)   the

"There's somebody \in it. Somebody who makes

($)strane

strange noises."

($)Antoe's   *wi-i-i-ide*

Antone's eyes opened wide. "It might be a giant!" he said. "Let's tell Saburo."

Fia's substitution of "the" for "it," which she immediately corrects, is the best evidence in her reading of this passage of how well she controls English. She probably predicted "in the house," and the author could as easily have said that instead of "in it." Fia is monitoring herself, and when she realizes the text isn't what she expects, she corrects. This is a beautiful example of how miscues show reading strengths, not just problems or weaknesses.

If we doubted that Fia is comprehending, she shows it with the special intonation she uses when she says "strane" for "strange." She gives it an eerie feeling. A little further along in the text Saburo says, "You mean the spooky one?" when told about the house, and Fia uses intonation to make that word sound spooky. Oral storytelling is important in Samoan culture and Fia brings narrative devices she has already learned into her reading of English.

In Hawaiian pidgin one can emphasize or extend the meaning of an adjective by elongating an internal vowel. That's why I used several <i>s in showing how she said "wide." In her rendition, his eyes open really wide, not just a little wide.

Is Fia making sense of this story? No doubt about it. We can't know from this reading how complete her understanding is, or whether it differs from the author's or our own, but we certainly know she is getting the undercurrent of excitement about a mysterious house. Her miscues demonstrate her competence as a reader of English, her second language. And the retelling that follows confirms her comprehension. Like Angela, Fia is acting like a competent user of language, constructing meaning as she reads. Like Angela, she is increasing her reading ability as she reads. And like Angela, she uses both her developing language competence and her knowledge of her world.

I chose these readers from among hundreds who have been taped reading texts they hadn't seen before. Each is different, and yet they are also all the same. What they do is what all readers must do to make sense of print — construct meaning as they read. All of them use the three cue systems: the signal (graphophonic), syntactic (lexico-grammatical), and semantic-pragmatic. They all sample from the print, make predictions and draw inferences, monitor their own reading, confirm or disconfirm their predictions and inferences, and self-correct as necessary. That is, they are all using the same reading process as you did and always do.

Longer portions of their reading and/or more readers would only provide more evidence. If you doubt that these readers are doing what all readers do, you can tape some readers yourself. Pick a story you think will be somewhat difficult for them and tape them reading the whole thing. Don't interrupt or offer help! Afterwards, ask them to retell the story they read, and finally, look carefully at a copy of the text as you listen to their oral reading on tape.

Summary

When Copernicus suggested that the Earth is a satellite of the sun rather than the center of the universe, he didn't change reality. As we stand here on Earth, the sun and moon and stars all seem to travel around us. What Copernicus and others taught us is that we need to look beyond the superficial "facts" for a more accurate and more useful explanation of what seems to be self-evident.

Today's "Copernican revolution" in the understanding of reading starts with a new respect for language, and for children as language learners who have already learned to make sense of oral language (in one or more languages) before they come to school, and who use their language competence in learning to make sense of written language. In the pre-Copernican world of understanding reading we thought accurate, rapid letter and/or word recognition was the center of the process and somehow comprehension followed. But now we know that reading is making sense of print, and that we can use the miscues readers produce as windows on the reading process.

6

*Written
text is a dynamic
organism; we must always
study it as a living
entity.*

How written text works

Reading, we've agreed, is a transaction between a reader and a text. We've already looked at the transactional nature of reading for both children and adults, but it's also important to understand the components of a written text, to understand how written texts provide cue systems for their readers.

This will be a long chapter and I can't help it. In fact, I could include a lot more information about different aspects of written text, but I don't want to overload you with more than you care to know about topics like English orthography, systemic-functional grammar, or discourse and text analysis. I do want to give you enough sense of texts to see how their nature influences the reading and writing processes.

The first and most important thing to keep in mind is this: like the human body, written text is a vibrant, dynamic organism. We can study its systems and components — what it does and can do, how it grows and adapts. But taking it apart and studying it when it's dead may give us false understandings, because the living whole is much more than the sum of its parts and systems. Written text, though it appears fixed and inactive, is in fact a complete, active, living entity. A writer uses the systems of his or her language to represent ideas, experiences, social relationships, and social and personal understandings and beliefs, all within a social and cultural context. The reader can transact with the writer's text on a number of levels because he or she shares the writer's knowledge of the common features, forms and systems of language.

In chapter three we looked at texts as functional wholes *within different social contexts*. In this chapter we'll look at the systems of language that function at different levels *within texts*. How these systems work together in a given text is very important for our understanding of reading, as, for instance, some knowledge of the human circulatory system is important for our understanding of the body. Remove it from the body, and all we have is a mess of veins, arteries and blood. In life, however, the circulatory system works with the respiratory system, the digestive system, and all the other systems to perform the functions of a living body. So it is with language systems.

Consider these two street signs:

New York City: **Curb your dog!**

Brighton, England: **Notice! £50 fine for persons permitting their dogs to foul the footpath by depositing their excrement thereon.**

Aside from the fact that the cultural contexts demand one type of sign in New York and another in Brighton, even though they serve the same purpose, there are a number of similarities and differences in these two texts.

Similarities

- ➤ They use the Roman alphabet, English words, and English grammar and syntax (sentence structure).
- ➤ They represent a message appropriate to the context in which the text is displayed (a sign beside a sidewalk/footpath).
- ➤ They are cohesive (they stick together in ways that make the text authentic).
- ➤ They are complete (although they don't explicitly state the complete message).
- ➤ They assume that readers will bring their experience to the reading.

Differences

These signs, and others like them, reflect the cultural context in the language choices their creators make:

- ➤ They select from many different fonts or type faces.
- ➤ They may use different spellings (*curb* is a verb here, but as a noun it would be *kerb* in Britain).
- ➤ They use different genres to achieve the same function (the New York sign is a simple command; the Brighton one more like a legal notice).

➤ They select different words, phrases and idioms which are determined, at least partly, by the choice of genre.

➤ They use different sentence structures, depending on the genre (in the sign genre, for instance, certain deletions are permitted — like "There is a" before "£50").

➤ They take into account the experiences and understandings readers are likely to bring to the reading (different for different countries — for that matter, the extent to which signs like these are obeyed is also a matter of culture and custom).

Each of these signs contains authentic text. Each is complete, as complete for its type as a novel is for its type. Each has all the required systems and levels of language, a function and purpose, and the potential for an intended audience to make sense of it.

Neither text, however, will be comprehended by readers who bring insufficient experience and meaning to it. Urban Tucson doesn't have sidewalks, and we don't accept the idea that the street beyond the curb is an appropriate (or legal) place for dog droppings — our dog owners have to carry pooper-scoopers. And no doubt there are many young English readers who won't know what's meant by "depositing their excrement."

On the other hand, as we saw earlier, non-alphabetic cues can sometimes be as useful for arriving at meaning as text. I came across the scene in this picture in Scandinavia. The context, the dog icon and the receptacle next to the sign made its message clear to me even though I couldn't read the text.

Language levels

Let's look now at the levels of language and the cue systems available to readers as they work at making sense of written texts, as shown in the following diagram:

Language Levels and Cue Systems in Oral and Written Language

Meaning and pragmatics

Experiential/ideational meaning   Context of situation
Interpersonal meaning   Cultural pragmatics
Textual meaning

Lexico-grammar

Syntax   Wording
    Pattern   Form
    Inflection   Frequency
    Pattern markers: function words   Arrangement

Graphophonics: the signal level

Oral Text   *Written Text*
Phonology   Orthography
    Sound system   (Phonics)   Spelling system
    Intonation   Punctuation

This chart is two-dimensional to make it possible to lay out on paper the language levels and their components. But if, instead, I could use a three-dimensional ball to represent language, the graphophonic (signal) level would be on the outside, the only level visible. The lexico-grammar level would be next to it inside, and at the core would be meaning and pragmatics.

Graphophonic level: orthography and perception

The letter patterns are observable signals our brains use in forming perceptions.

Although the chart shows the "meaning and pragmatics" level at the top, we'll begin our discussion with the graphophonic level. For two reasons, I've begun to call this the *signal* level:

➤ It refers to what we can actually see or hear. Our brain relies on *audible and visual signals* to get the information it uses to form perceptions.

➤ It also refers to a system of signs capable of being interpreted by and having a value assigned by the brain. What we see and hear is not just sensory input but a *semiotic system:* signs to be interpreted.

Reading and listening begin with the brain's perception of an observable signal — sounds and/or characters or letters. This signal is the only part of language that has physical characteristics that can be observed and, therefore, measured, studied and described. For instance, scientists can study not only the characteristics of sounds: frequency, pitch, duration, etc. (acoustic phonetics), but also the way speakers use the various organs of the mouth to produce those sounds (articulatory phonetics).

In the same way, we can study orthography, the physical characteristics of writing that the eye provides as signals for the brain to use in building perceptions — not only what the characters look like, but also how they are produced and how they fit together.

Discrete sounds and letters aren't the only signals the brain uses, however. Oral language uses intonation as well. Intonation is a characteristic of a *stream* of language, not of any one sound; it rides above the component sounds. Similarly, written language is not simply a string of letters. It is patterned in complex ways and punctuated to represent wording, grammar and meaning. Remember our discussion about how readers transact with text, however. The characteristics of written texts are very much determined both by how they are produced and how they are comprehended. If those characteristics had made creating and understanding texts difficult for us, they would have changed long ago.

One extraordinary thing about the signal level in both oral and written language is that the signal — what we see and what we hear — is ambiguous. Neither the sound system nor the orthography is exact or even close to constant. And that's a good thing, because if every sound or letter had to be perfectly produced, an exact match for every letter or sound, always the same in every human context, then communication through language would be impossibly hard work. In fact, we humans have a remarkable ability to deal with ambiguity — "a set for ambiguity" I've come to call it. We assign what we hear and/or see to perceptual schemas we've built, and continue to build, in our minds. And we do this with relative ease, since we know things fit in only a limited number of perceptual categories, and since we can draw on information from the other language levels to resolve ambiguity at the signal level.

You'll notice that in my chart phonics appears between phonology and orthography. Because I define phonics as *the set of relationships between the orthography and a specific speaker's phonology*, I've also put phonics in parentheses. It isn't part of either language system; instead, it's a system of *correspondences* between sound and spelling systems, assigned by each reader of an alphabetically written language as perception takes place. In other words, the phonic relationships between the two systems are also ambiguous.

Much discussion of phonics is based on the naïve assumption that individual letters are recognized and matched with a single sound, and the sounds are blended into syllables and words, which are then recognized. And finally, somehow, each string of words is comprehended. That kind of recognition of letters and words would imply a brain with templates to recognize and identically match every form. What the eye sees and what the ear hears are not precise forms, however, but a myriad of variable sounds and shapes. The brain does something much more complex and wonderful than recognizing letters and matching them to sounds. It creates perceptions from the ambiguous signals it receives, building order out of ambiguous information.

We'll come to how it does that (see also *Phonics Phacts*), but first let's look at the various forms of signal (graphophonic) ambiguity readers have to cope with.

Letter and sound ambiguity

Think of a young baby waking to the morning voice-sounds of a household: siblings' voices high-pitched, father's deep, mother's higher-pitched again but mature, radio newscaster's carefully modulated. Using all this input, the baby will invent her own sound system. Constrained by the articulatory system, she will sort out what is to be perceived as the same in all this difference and learn to treat as different what even by scientific measurements is the same. Early on, her own speech sounds will fall outside the family's range, and yet she will be understood if she says anything even close to what she's intending to say because of her family's *set for ambiguity*, enhanced by their celebration of her attempts at language use. Some early inventions will become part of the "familiolect," like my oldest daughter's invention of "bottom" for "blanket," and her three-year-old sister's renaming of "Fisherman's Dwarf" and "Lake Taco" as she transformed what she heard into what made sense to her.

As the child keeps striving to understand and be understood, her personal phonology, though unique, will come to fall within the ranges of her family's. She'll be speaking their dialect, or more precisely their familiolect — the particular variant of the community dialect her family is evolving. She and all others in her language community will perceive the speech of each as alike in significant ways, although differences would be obvious to an observer.

Now let's look at the orthography — the writing system — which those members of her family who are literate in English use. After my book *Phonics Phacts* had been published, I realized it would have been interesting if the cover had contained the title printed in many different fonts.

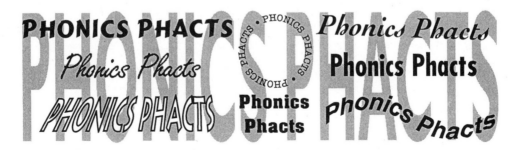

These are only a few of the many fonts available. They all "say the same thing," right? In reality, they don't say anything, of course. But we readers of English have learned to treat these very different graphic displays as if they are all the same, and we construct the same meaning from them.

Take a good look at the differences. Many of the <p>s look alike . . . or do they? The <h>s differ a lot more. And look at all the different <a>s! Some of the fonts join the letters, some space them equally, some mash them together. Linguists say that we select distinctive features in assigning sounds or shapes, but there are no constant features for any one letter. And it doesn't matter. Letters are really perceptual categories. There is no real <a>. There are many different shapes we learn to treat as the mental construct "a" in appropriate contexts.

Let me restate a point I'll be making throughout this discussion: the way we write letters is highly variable, even though within a given print font the letters take the same shapes (capitals and small letters) throughout. In handwriting we're much less consistent, of course; we all have our own idiosyncrasies. You may be surprised to discover that you actually leave a lot of the letter parts (and sometimes even letters) out as you write at a comfortable speed. But remember, making sense of print doesn't require uniformity in letters and sounds. Our wonderful minds can handle all that ambiguity — if they couldn't, our writing systems wouldn't exist. Ambiguity is a good thing: not only would writing be next to impossible if we all had to produce invariant forms for the letters, it would be incredibly dull. The multitude of fonts in use serve to make what we read more aesthetically pleasing, more comfortable to read, more suitable for different contexts and functions. Imagine a wedding invitation looking like a billboard or a court summons! Imagine a newspaper printed in a single font and size!

It wasn't just a joke that I spelled "facts" with <ph> instead of <f> in the title of *Phonics Phacts*. I wanted to call attention to the fact that even in the word *phonics*, single graphemes do not represent single phonemes. Both <f> and <ph> occur in the spellings of words that begin with the /f/ phoneme. (Linguists use the term grapheme for a significant unit of written language, just as they use phoneme for a significant unit of oral language. Graphemes and phonemes are perceptual units. Our minds have constructed one schema for graphemes, another for phonemes.)

Pattern ambiguity

English is an alphabetically written language and, by definition, alphabetic writing is a system in which the sound system is represented in the writing system. The naïve version of that is that letters represent sounds. Even in more scientific discussions, we sometimes hear the phrase "phoneme-grapheme correspondences." But there can be no *simple* one-to-one correspondence in any alphabetically written language. Always the relationships, which are more complex in English because of its multiple roots in Germanic, Romance and other languages, must be between sound *patterns* and written *patterns*. And that's because sound systems and graphic systems work differently; they simply can't match item for item.

As complex as English spelling looks, it is really quite orderly and patterned. One very common pattern is demonstrated in word pairs like <m><a><n> and <m><a><n><e>. Many single-syllable words composed of three sounds in a consonant-vowel-consonant pattern have word partners that differ only in that the vowels can be long or short. The spelling system handles that by adding an <e> after the second consonant to indicate a long vowel sound. *Man* and *mane* fit that pattern, as do *pan/pane, van/vane, mat/mate, rat/rate*, etc.

Before we go ahead, let me point out that this final <e> is no more or less silent than any other letter. None of them "say" anything. What is special is that here a letter is being used as a *marker* — which, incidentally, means the letters can't be read sequentially from left to right! The whole pattern, including the <e> ending, must be processed to decide which word it is and how it will be pronounced. Actually, in context, the <e> usually simply confirms what has already been predicted in the course of reading the whole text.

Now think about *main* and *Maine*, which are homophones (sound-alikes) for *mane*, at least in my dialect. There are many words that fit this consonant-*ai*-consonant pattern to create long-*a* words: *pain, gait, rail, maid, pair*, etc. But notice also *feign, deign, reign* and *Wayne* and *Jayne*. And one more pattern that fits the short vowel pattern in a multi-syllable word: *manic, panic, satanic*, etc. *Maniac*, on the other hand, has a long vowel!

There is some value in having contrasting patterns of spelling for homophones like *mane/main/Maine, pane/pain/Paine,* and *pare/pair/pear*. However, we also have homographs like *read/read* and *lead/lead* that are spelled the same although pronounced differently. And in some pairs, like *record/record* and *desert/desert*, nouns and verbs are spelled the same but shift the stress.

That brings us back to our refrain: these pattern ambiguities would have disappeared if they made reading and writing impossible or even very difficult. But we easily treat spellings that are the same as different and spellings that are different as the same. For example, read this paragraph:

> The <u>main</u> feature of the <u>male</u> lion is its <u>red</u> <u>mane</u>. I <u>read</u> about that in a book I got in the <u>mail</u> last week. I <u>like</u> to <u>read</u> books <u>like</u> that.

It shouldn't surprise you that you had no particular difficulty with the underlined words. In the context of the syntax and meaning of the text, the pattern ambiguities are disambiguated. In normal reading you are scarcely aware that there is any ambiguity.

Schwa and stress ambiguity

Perhaps the most remarkable ambiguity of English spelling results from a language change in England in the fourteenth century. All unaccented vowels became a common vowel, usually called *schwa* and represented by linguists as /ə/. In "I am a man and my name is Goodman," the vowel in *man* is a short *a* (/æ/), but in the second syllable of my name, which is unstressed, it becomes /ə/. Sometimes people hear my name as "Goodwin" because the vowel in *win* is also a schwa. Here's the dilemma. Should we spell the same word in two ways, one when the vowel is stressed and another when it's unstressed, or should the spelling remain constant, using the spelling of the stressed form? We chose the latter option for our spelling system, and so we spell *man* the same even though the vowel changes to schwa in the unstressed syllable.

Earlier I said th<u>a</u>t *can* fits th<u>e</u> same short-*a* patt<u>er</u>n as *man*. B<u>u</u>t c<u>o</u>nsider th<u>i</u>s sent<u>e</u>nce: *I c<u>a</u>n reach th<u>e</u> can <u>o</u>f paint <u>o</u>n th<u>e</u> shelf.* As <u>a</u> funct<u>io</u>n w<u>o</u>rd, th<u>e</u> f<u>i</u>rst *can* <u>i</u>n the sent<u>e</u>nce is unstressed so it goes t<u>o</u> schwa <u>a</u>nd sounds like "kin." B<u>u</u>t th<u>e</u> noun lat<u>er</u> <u>i</u>n th<u>e</u> sent<u>e</u>nce gets full stress <u>a</u>nd full vow<u>e</u>l. Funct<u>io</u>n w<u>o</u>rds usu<u>a</u>lly are unstressed. And since funct<u>io</u>n w<u>o</u>rds are very comm<u>o</u>n, this pract<u>i</u>ce of keep<u>i</u>ng th<u>e</u> spelling const<u>a</u>nt ev<u>e</u>n when th<u>e</u> vow<u>e</u>l shifts t<u>o</u> schw<u>a</u> is very comm<u>o</u>n.

(I underlined the unstressed vowels in the previous paragraph to show how common they are. Notice that they are spelled with every vowel, as well as combinations of vowels.)

Advocates of direct phonics instruction often use a list of single-syllable words to teach phonics out of context. But in a list, every single-syllable word has the same strong stress, so there are no schwas. Words of more than one syllable are more problematic, since one or more syllables will be unstressed, as in "Goodman." *Syllable* itself is an interesting word: the second syllable is unstressed, so the <a> represents the schwa, but in *syllabic*, the <y> represents the schwa. Even *phonics* has a schwa in the second syllable. Schwas everywhere, except in phonics instruction!

In many Latin-based English words, the spelling remains the same but the stress shifts when the word changes from noun to verb: *record/record, contract/ contract, desert/desert, produce/produce*, etc. Consider also how stress (and schwa) shifts in these words *cónvent/convéntion/ convéntional/ conventionálity*.

This schwa ambiguity is more of a problem for writers than for readers. When we read, we use our knowledge of the stress rules in perceiving the spelling patterns and relating them to the sound patterns. But in writing, it's hard to predict which vowel will appear in an unstressed syllable, since it could be any. In some patterns, such as words ending in <ent> and <ant> (*independent, relevant*), there is no rule for deciding.

Still, readers learn to handle the ambiguity. Using data from a study of native American children in southern Arizona, Goodman and Wilde (1992) reported that after two years (third and fourth grades) a group of children spelled stressed short vowels 94.4% conventionally. In story contexts, unstressed vowels were 74% conventionally spelled in the third grade and 83% in the fourth. Since phonics is of no help in predicting how any particular unstressed oral vowel will appear in spelling, the accomplishments of these children must result from other inputs: extensive reading, familiarity with how words look, and familiar patterns across words.

Morphophonemic ambiguity

Spelling rules reflect meaning and sound.

The spelling of vowels in stressed and unstressed syllables relates to the more general issue of sound changes at the word and morpheme level of English. *Morphemics* refers to how morphemes, the meaning-structure units of language, combine to make words; the changes in sounds as morphemes come together are called *morphophonemics*. Some sounds change as other sounds follow them, partly because the parts of the mouth used to produce certain sounds need to change shape or position when certain other sounds follow.

Morphophonemics is a bit more complex than that, however. Notice what happens to consonants in these related words:

➤ In *please/pleasure*, we go from /z/ to /ž/, but the spelling remains <s>. *Measure* and *treasure* have the same sound sequence.

➤ In *confess/confession, press/pressure, compress/compression*, the <ss> remains but the sound goes to /š/. *Issue* and *tissue* are the same.

➤ In *race/racial, space/spacial, face/facial*, the <c> spelling is retained although the sound shifts to /š/.

➤ In *rite/ritual, site/situate, fact/factual* and other words that end in a /t/ sound, that sound changes to /č/ before certain vowels.

➤ In words like *situate/situation, inflate/inflation, state/station, educate/education, intent/intention, rate/ration*, the <t> is retained in the spelling but the sound becomes /š/. But notice that *tense* goes to *tension* although *mention* uses the <t> spelling.

This type of ambiguity results from decisions made in standardizing spelling to keep meaning relationships clear by having related words spelled consistently even though sounds change in the derived forms. Spelling, then, doesn't simply reflect how words sound, but also what they mean.

A similar standardization occurs in some grammatical features, particularly with the past tense morpheme and the *s* forms of verbs and nouns. In oral English, the past tense morpheme has three alternate forms, or *allomorphs*, depending on the final consonant sound in the base form of the verb. Notice that the spelling always remains <ed> (unless the vowel shifts too, and then the spelling goes to <t>: *slept, kept*).

➤ /ɨd/ as in *wanted, waded;*

➤ /d/ as in *grabbed, lagged, raged, baled, tamed, rained;*

➤ /t/ as in *walked, stepped, taped, lacked, waxed.*

An *s* form is used for the plural of English nouns and the third person singular of present tense verbs. Again there are three allomorphs, depending on the final consonants of the base forms. Here the most common spelling is <s>, although /ɨz/ is usually <es>.

➤ /ɨz/ as in *glasses, cases, boxes, mazes, races, razes, praises;*

➤ /s/ as in *likes, muffs, tops, tapes, ticks* and in all words ending in the /f/ sound: *laughs, graphs;*

➤ /z/ as in *robs, robes, beds, begs, bales, hams, tans, bats, waves.*

Because these morphophonemic shifts are so predictable in the sound system of English, the spelling ambiguity is resolved at the syntactic level. The morpheme is spelled more consistently than it's pronounced.

Dialect and rule ambiguity

The tendency to standardize spelling across forms relates to the most important of all aspects of signal ambiguity in English spelling: dialect ambiguity.

As the printing press made possible mass production of relatively cheap copies of books, newspapers and other written texts, printers were confronted with a major problem. Every language is actually a family of related regional and social dialects, which vary from each other in their phonology (and all other levels). Either the printers would have to print a version of each text for each dialect community, or spelling would have to be standardized across dialects. By 1755, when Samuel Johnson's dictionary was published, most spellings in England had become standardized, although monument inscriptions show varied spellings well into the next century. In America, Noah Webster, supported by important American literary figures, deliberately introduced into his 1829 dictionary a number of spellings that differed from the British. That's why modern American spelling differs notably from British.

The decision to standardize spelling introduced a major source of ambiguity for all speakers. Remember, I defined phonics as the set of relationships between the orthography and the phonology *of a particular speaker* of the language. Phonics relationships vary from speaker to speaker and dialect to dialect, and there is no single set of rules that fit all of us. Furthermore, the correspondences aren't neatly related in different dialects.

Look at these words all spelled with <og> in English. As I pronounce them, there are two different vowels:

➤ /o/: *bog, cog, grog, smog, tog, flog*

➤ /ɔ/: *dog, fog, frog, hog, log*

Notice that my *fog* rhymes with *dog*, but my *smog* rhymes with *cog*. Some dialects don't have the "open o" (my second list), so for them all of the words would rhyme. Most North Americans do have two different vowels, although they might not list these words in the same way I do. We find the same difference/non-difference in words like *cot/caught* and *tot/taught*, but in these there is a spelling difference as well.

Do your *almonds* have an /l/ sound? What about *palm*? *Help*? In Stillwater, Oklahoma, *help* is a two-syllable word sounding to me like *hey-ulp*. A favorite of linguists is the difference among American dialects in the pronunciation of *Mary, merry* and *marry*. For me those all sound the same, but in some dialects all three are different, and in some two are the same and one is not. How do these line up for you: *root, roof, room*? Does your *root* sound like your *route*? Mine does. But my *roof* has the same vowel sound as in *good*. Which of these are homophones for you: *bin, been, bean, Ben, being*? Isn't this fun? Unfortunately it's anything but fun for kids who are being told that their reading is wrong because they're rendering words in their own dialect.

There's a lot of research evidence that, as young learners begin reading and writing, they invent spellings to match the way they say and hear words in their own dialect and then gradually become aware that conventional, standardized spellings don't match their inventions. The rules they've invented get them close, but they have to learn the conventional spellings mostly through their reading.

The set for ambiguity

What we've learned in this section is that what we actually see in written language (the signal) is not a simple and constant set of letters or spelling patterns but a very ambiguous display. And not only does this ambiguous written language system relate to an equally ambiguous oral language system, the relationship itself is complexly ambiguous. My reason for stressing the ambiguity is to highlight the remarkable human capacity for dealing with it. In fact, text is ambiguous *because* we are capable of making sense of it.

We humans have a set for ambiguity. However, although the information we get from the graphophonic signal is ambiguous, the perceptions we form from it are not. When we work to make sense of the text, we:

➤ use schemas to guide our expectations and form our perceptions;

➤ perceive things that are different as the same;

➤ perceive things that are the same as different;

➤ perceive things differently in different contexts;

➤ use alternate information sources to resolve ambiguity;

➤ use minimal information to get to meaning.

We resolve ambiguity with information from the other language levels, and we'll turn to those now. In the next chapter we'll come back to perceptions and cues.

Lexico-grammar level: syntax and wording

You can't use language to communicate without having to use its grammar.

Grammar is the structure of language. Syntax is the grammar of sentences, and since most grammar is about sentences, syntax and grammar often seem to be synonymous.

Let me first bring a ghost out of the closet. I know from experience that many of you are already trying to decide whether to skip this section on grammar. Unpleasant memories haunt you — drills, diagraming and, for a "lucky" few, tree diagrams. But here's the good news: each of you is already an expert in the use of the grammar of at least one language. You can't use language to communicate without using its grammar. Language without grammar would be incomprehensible.

What makes you uncomfortable is having to talk about grammar abstractly in technical language. There's a big difference between being an expert user of language — a master of grammar — and being an expert grammarian, able to analyze and discuss the structure of language. The funny thing is that even the best grammarians haven't been able to explain everything expert grammar users do in their daily use of language.

So, hang in as we get into this section. All I want to do is make clear how readers and writers use their knowledge of grammar. I won't promise to relieve a lifetime of school-induced grammar anxiety totally, but I do promise to use real language examples to make the terms clear. And maybe when we're done you'll appreciate yourself a little more as a grammarian.

Sentence patterns

See Spot run!

This sentence from the Scott-Foresman basal of the 1930s has passed into North American folklore. Many adults remember it from the early days of their learning how to read. It's firmly established in humor and folklore as representative of the primer genre, and has found it's way into cartoons, T-shirts, and pop-art.

Let's start our discussion about how syntax and grammar work in reading by analyzing the structure of that three-word sentence. We'll see how readers must use syntax in making sense of print, and while we're at it, we'll look at the grammar differences between artificial and authentic texts.

When we looked at the "Mardsan Giberter" text (p.43), I pointed out how powerfully our knowledge of English syntax contributes to making sense even of nonsense. We noted also that English syntax depends strongly on patterns like subject-verb-object *(She had just sparved the binky)* or subject-copula-adjective *(Glis was very fraper)*.

Now, back to *See Spot run!* I should explain to non-North Americans that *Spot* is a dog visible in the accompanying illustration. I'll explain later why his name had to be Spot and not Fido or Rin-tin-tin.

The sentence starts with a verb and seems to have an unusual verb-noun-verb pattern. Furthermore, the object of the verb *see* isn't the noun *Spot*, but the clause *Spot run*. This three-word sentence actually has two clauses! One serves as the object of the verb in the main clause, but where's the subject? Who is supposed to do the seeing? It turns out that this is a command — someone is telling someone to see Spot run. You may remember some of your teachers telling you that in commands (also known as imperatives) the subject is an understood *you* — something I never really understood until I took a graduate course in linguistics.

The sentence is really: *(You) see Spot run.* In fact, in the original primer the page says: *Father! See Spot run!* This *you* (understood) is in reality *father*, although that word isn't in the command. In linguistic terms, *you* and *father* have the same referent, a person who is the father of the speaker.

Ready for the next syntactic problem with this not-so-simple three-word sentence? Shouldn't the verb *run*, which has *Spot* as its subject, have an <s> on it, since *Spot* is a third-person singular noun? Not really. You see, this *run* isn't an ordinary verb but an infinitive. So shouldn't it be *to run*? Well, no. In English there are times when an infinitive drops the *to* after certain other verbs. We say: "Tell Spot to run" or "Get Spot to run" but also "Make Spot run" or "Have Spot run." (Some Southerners say "Have Spot to run.") Why does it work this way?

I don't know! It's another of those ambiguities, this time on a phrase level — one of many exceptions to the syntactic rules.

So, the sentence is actually *(You) see Spot (to) run.* Transformational grammarians might say that *you* and *to* are in the deep structure but deleted from the surface structure. (I'll use the distinction between surface and deep structure a few more times. By deep structure I mean the underlying structure of the sentence; surface structure refers to what is represented visually.)

Ironically, none of this complexity is what really makes this three-word sentence hard to read. Kids, even the six-year-olds this is intended for, are quite familiar with imperatives:

> Shut your mouth! Pick up your clothes! Go to sleep! Eat your dinner! Make him stop! Sit down!

Kids hear those commands all the time and have no problem making sense of them. But they don't often hear "see" as a command. The authors/editors chose an inappropriate verb! They could have said "Look at Spot run!" or "Look at Spot go!" or "Watch Spot run," but "See Spot run" wasn't a good choice.

What's worse, since the usual cue for predicting that a sentence is a command is that it starts with the simple form (no endings) of the verb, confusion reigns when the right form is in the right spot but the verb is wrong. Not surprisingly, many young readers produced this miscue: "Father sees Spot run." They took *father* from the preceding text and made it the subject, then made *see* into *sees* to fit the third-person singular subject and presto!, they had a nice subject-verb-object sentence. This miscue demonstrates that readers *assign a syntactic pattern to the text as they read*. They use their knowledge of grammar to predict a sensible text and produce one. By putting a ¿ or a ¡ at the beginning of questions or exclamations, Spanish acknowledges the point I've been making, that all readers and speakers predict the syntax of each sentence as it begins.

Why, then, did this team of authors and editors — experts on reading — include this unfortunate sentence in their primer? The answer is that they:

➤ weren't paying much attention to grammar because they didn't understand how important it is for texts to be authentic, or how authentic grammar is used in making sense of texts;

➤ didn't give kids credit for controlling the grammar and using it in their reading.

These and other basal makers worked from the premise that *language is a bunch of words* and *learning to read is learning words*. They chose words on the basis of frequency in the language rather than in a particular authentic text. They created inauthentic, non-cohesive, sometimes ungrammatical and frequently unpredictable texts, often using the wrong words in the wrong places. Their behavioral learning theory made them believe that every word is learned separately, so *see* and *sees*, *run* and *runs* are all distinct words that have to be learned separately. They aren't. Readers simply choose the form appropriate to the syntax they've assigned to the sentence. If *father* is the subject, then *sees* must be the verb. Wording and syntax work together and words take alternate forms depending on their syntactic function.

See was chosen by the basal makers rather than *look at* or *watch*, both more predictable in this command form, because *see* had to be repeated once it was introduced. Readers who try to make sense of this unpredictable and inauthentic text use their knowledge of syntax and thus make miscues. Those who focus only on getting the words right produce different miscues (perhaps phonic near misses like *stop* for *Spot*) but don't get the sense.

Artificial texts that control word frequency and disrupt authentic sentence structures don't provide readers with cues for predicting and expecting. Authentic texts, on the other hand, not only control their own vocabulary but also have predictable, authentic grammar and thus provide natural grammatical cues for readers.

In chapter five we saw that even second-language learners reveal their knowledge of the syntax of the language as they read, as Fia did when she predicted *in the house* for *in it*. In fact, research shows that second-language learners who are already literate in another language learn English grammar in the course of learning to make sense of texts. Reading is often the earliest of the four language processes they come to control.

One other thing before we leave this famous three-word, two-clause sentence: I promised to tell you why the dog is called Spot (and why the cat in the same series is called Puff). Once again the creators' incorrect views — that language is a bunch of words that occur with variable frequency and that learning to read is learning words through repeated exposure — come into play in their choice of real words for the names of animals, characters and even places. *Spot* might be owned by the *Park* family and live on *Cherry* Street in *River* Town. That assumes that sheer repetition of the word produces learning, and grammatical function and meaning don't matter.

Miscue research shows a quite different pattern. In a story about a circus coming to town, young readers produced far fewer miscues on *circus* used as a noun, as in *The circus is coming,* than when it appeared as a noun modifier, as in *He liked the circus clowns.* They found it easier to read *vines* in *He hid in the rose vines* than in *Mr. Vines' candy store.* Miscues were more likely on *river* in *He lived in River Town* than in *He fell into the river.* Children combine their knowledge of grammar and wording to make sense of text. When grammar and wording information seem unconnected, comprehending is harder and miscues are more likely to occur. What do vines have do with candy stores?

Word frequency

Overall frequency of words doesn't matter as much as the frequency in specific texts.

In the first quarter of the 20th century, a lot of effort went into making education scientific. Those concerned with finding a scientific basis for reading instruction were much taken with finding "laws of learning" and creating highly controlled text materials to fit those laws. They thought they could create such perfect instructional texts that they would overcome the handicaps of minimally educated teachers. Edward Thorndike, a leader in all that, developed a small number of laws of learning rooted in behavioral psychology and then looked for ways to control reading instruction. It dawned on him and others that, since some words appear all the time and some are very rare, what they needed was controlled vocabulary. If reading was learning words, then young readers should learn the most frequent words first. So they gathered huge sets of language texts (one study used several consecutive issues of the Buffalo NY Sunday newspaper) and counted every word, creating lists in frequency order — a laborious job in a time before computers.

Thorndike published his first list under the title: *The Teacher's Word Book* (1921). William S. Gray (1919, 1925) and others used it to build the first modern basal readers, based on these key premises:

➤ start by introducing only the most frequent words;

➤ repeat those words frequently to assure they are learned;

➤ use frequent words whenever possible in place of infrequent ones.

They produced a new genre, the basal primer, with such a small number of words that pictures had to carry the story. Publishers fell all over themselves to produce material with fewer and fewer words, developing as many as three pre-primers to precede the primers. *See Spot run* is typical pre-primer language.

But word frequency is *not* a phenomenon independent of the text in which it occurs. These "scientific" researchers didn't recognize the factors that really determine the wording of any particular text. They looked on word frequency as a cause of text difficulty, not as a product of text requirements. In my own research on word frequency, I found that in any text a small number of words, about 25, account for around 40% of all the words in that text: *the*, for example, can itself make up 10%, since most nouns require an article. (Since definite nouns take *the* and usually the majority of nouns are definite, *the* is more common than the indefinite *a*.)

About half of the most frequent words in any story are function words: determiners like *the*, prepositions, conjunctions, auxiliary verbs or copulas (mostly *be* forms), and pronouns. These words show up on Thorndike's list as frequent, of course, but they have little meaning in themselves and are best learned in context.

It's the other half of the most frequent words in any story that are in question, and these are frequent *because of the plot and characters of the particular story* — some of them may be far down on Thorndike's frequent words list. First-person stories contain many uses of *I, me, my* and *mine*. If the main characters are female, *she, her, hers* will be common. In one story we used in our research the central character is Peggy, a sheep dog who has to protect her flock from coyotes. Can you guess which words are most common in that text? *Sheep* and *coyote* aren't included in any of the high-frequency lists, however. Nor is *ewe*, but after reading that story almost every reader could tell us what a ewe is — although few were sure how to pronounce it. On the other hand, most of the less common words in a text occur only once. They usually aren't very important to comprehending the text, and readers can easily infer their meanings from the syntactic and semantic context.

The table on the following page shows the word frequency data on three of the stories we've used in our research. (For your information, story 53 has a total of 2030 running words and 645 different words; story 59 has 3667 and 952; story 60, 4208 and 883.) What can you tell about the plot and cast of characters just by knowing the most frequent words?

Twelve words are among the most common in all three stories: *the, and, to, a, of, in, it, that, at, he, for, on. It* and *he* are pronouns; the rest are function words that help to shape the structure of each story. The high frequency verbs and nouns in each of the lists are there because of the specific story lines. S59, the sheep dog story, has these nouns: *Peggy* (the dog), *sheep, coyote, coyotes* and *band* (the band of sheep). *She* and *her* are each used 105 times because the main character, Peggy, is female. On the other hand, *said*, the only verb in the list of most common words in S53 and S60, isn't in the list for S59 — since the main characters are animals, it has almost no dialogue. Only one adjective, *typical*, makes the top 25 in any of the stories. A central aspect of the plot in S53 is that <u>Mr. Barnaby</u> thinks <u>Andrew</u> is a <u>typical</u> <u>baby</u>. The underlined words are among the most common in the story.

English has a rich vocabulary, partly due to our multiple language roots. For example, a lot of verbs with Latin roots have Germanic synonyms that use verb particles: *construct/build up, compose/make up, decompose/break down, omit/leave out, conclude/finish up, discern/make out, continue/carry on, inspect/look over*. And because we have so much choice, we tend to avoid repeating the same word.

Most Frequent Words in Three Stories

Rank	Story 53[1]	N	%	Cum.	Story 59[2]	N	%	Cum.	Story 60[3]	N	%	Cum.
1	The	82	3.9	3.9	the	370	9.9	9.9	the	259	6.0	6.0
2	I	80	3.9	7.8	and	116	3.1	13.0	and	166	3.8	9.8
3	a	65	3.1	10.9	to	110	2.9	15.9	he	137	3.1	12.9
4	and	52	2.5	13.4	she	105	2.8	18.7	I	123	2.8	15.7
5	he	51	2.4	15.8	her	105	2.8	21.5	to	117	2.7	18.4
6	said	51	2.4	18.2	of	100	2.6	24.1	it	90	2.0	20.4
7	to	48	2.3	21.5	a	76	2.0	26.1	his	85	1.9	22.3
8	you	31	1.5	23.0	was	62	1.6	27.7	was	82	1.9	24.2
9	Mr.	28	1.3	14.3	Peggy	40	1.0	28.7	a	78	1.8	26.0
10	my	28	1.3	25.6	it	36	.9	29.6	of	73	1.6	27.6
11	of	28	1.3	26.9	sheep	34	.9	30.5	in	58	1.3	28.9
12	baby	26	1.2	28.1	in	33	.9	31.3	Harry	45	1.0	29.9
13	Barnaby	25	1.2	29.3	for	33	.9	32.1	on	36	.8	30.7
14	at	24	1.1	30.4	had	31	.8	32.9	you	36	.8	31.5
15	was	24	1.1	31.5	as	31	.8	33.7	at	33	.7	32.2
16	Andrew	23	1.1	32.6	from	27	.7	34.4	that	31	.7	32.9
17	in	22	1.0	33.6	on	27	.7	35.1	me	30	.6	33.5
18	his	20	.9	34.5	coyote	24	.6	35.7	but	29	.6	34.1
19	it	19	.8	35.4	that	22	.5	36.2	him	29	.6	34.7
20	on	17	.6	36.2	at	21	.5	36.7	up	29	.6	35.3
21	as	14	.6	36.8	were	21	.5	37.2	there	28	.6	35.9
22	but	14	.6	37.4	he	20	.5	37.7	said	28	.6	36.5
23	for	14	.6	38.0	his	20	.5	38.2	now	26	.6	37.1
24	that	13	.6	38.6	down	19	.5	38.7	for	25	.6	37.6
25	typical	13	.6	39.2	into	18	.4	39.1	Ganderbai	25	.5	38.1
					coyotes	18	.4	39.5	my	25	.5	38.6
					band	18	.4	39.9	not	25	.5	39.1
									out	25	.5	39.6

[1] My Brother Is a Genius   [2] Sheep Dog   [3] Poison

So, at the beginning of S60 (see also pp.49-56), many words and phrases are used to describe the movement of the main character into the house: *drove, approached, opened, coming, parked, went up, take steps, got to, crossed, pushed through, went across*. Together, these different words form a cohesive chain that creates a meaning structure for the text. In another story with an island setting, there are 12 references to a canoe that figures prominently in the story, but only twice is the word *canoe* used.

My table doesn't show it, but over half of all the different words in each of the three stories occur only once in the text. These may be high or low in Thorndike's word list, but they can't be central to understanding this story if they occur only once.

My message is that when you control vocabulary you create artificial and unpredictable texts, whereas authentic texts control their own vocabulary. On the other hand, as we'll see in the next chapter, even uncommon words can be predictable in a given context.

Lexico-grammar level: syntactic cue systems

Several grammar systems provide readers (and listeners) with cues they use to construct the grammar of the text they are trying to make sense of. To a certain extent these systems are universals of language, but each language uses them in different ways and assigns different importance to them. We'll look at three: patterns, pattern markers and rules.

Patterns

Earlier we discussed the importance of sentence patterns. In English, those are fairly fixed: subjects come before verbs, adjectives before nouns, etc. Only a few features are movable — adverbs, for example:

He devoured the delicious food <u>ravenously</u>.

<u>Ravenously</u>, he devoured the delicious food.

He <u>ravenously</u> devoured the delicious food.

He devoured <u>ravenously</u> the delicious food.

Because English sentence patterns are relatively fixed, we predict them confidently as soon as we have any minimal cues. So, *Glis was very fraper* is assigned a common pattern from our first eye fixation.

Writers start with meaning, and a *clause* is the smallest text unit that can represent an expression of meaning. When your third-grade teacher taught you that a sentence is a complete thought, he or she was wrong. A sentence can contain one or many *somewhat* complete thoughts (clauses), joined and combined to relate them to each other and to the meaning of the text. Each clause itself has a structure, some variation of subject and predicate. It is at the deep structure level that meaning is represented by these clause structures.

The text an author produces must be unpacked syntactically so the reader can recognize the underlying clauses and how they're combined to represent meaning. As adult readers we do this casually in the process of making meaning. Lest you think this is a characteristic of complex texts written for adults only, however, let's "unpack" a text passage from a children's story.

"If you stay home to do my work, you'll have to make butter, carry water from the well, wash the clothes, clean the house, and look after the baby," said the wife.

"I can do all that," replied the husband.

This version of the familiar folktale "The Man Who Kept House" comes from a Canadian basal reader intended for grade three children. Notice that the complex sentence in this passage appears as a quotation, with the dialogue carrier — *said the wife* — appearing at the end, reversing the usual English subject-verb sequence.

Here's a breakdown of the clauses and the complex system of representing them in the text:

If you stay home	(If) you stay (at) home
to do my work	(you) (inf) do work (work is mine)
you'll have to make butter	(then) you'll have to make butter
carry water from the well	(then) you'll have to carry water from the well
clean the house	(then) you'll have to clean the house
and look after the baby	(then) you'll have to look after the baby

Since this sequence of clauses starts with an *If*, there is an implicit *then* not represented in the surface text (if x, then y). The verb in the second clause, *to do my work*, is an infinitive because the verb in the first clause is *stay*. It has the meaning of "for the purpose of" or "in order to": *You stay home in order to do my work*. What follows the implicit "then" is a series of clauses starting with *you'll have to make butter*. But a cohesion rule has been used by the writer that deletes the *you'll have to* from all but the first of the four parallel clauses — parallel because they have the same beginning and the same syntactic structure, a verb followed by an object.

I love this example because it shows that the prohibition against split infinitives is quite wrong. *Make, carry, clean* and *look* are all infinitives but the *to* that usually precedes infinitive verbs is only in the first clause, *you'll have <u>to</u> make butter.*

Our research readers often pause after *butter.* They seem to be trying to figure out why the next word, *carry,* is a verb. At that point, they may not yet have assigned a structure that can accommodate a series of parallel clauses that start with verbs. Once the series falls into place for them, their intonation tells us that they've assigned the appropriate syntactic structure to unpack these clauses.

Pattern markers

Function words and grammatical (inflectional) word endings mark the patterns of the sentences. In "Mardsan Giberter," the first part of the text would look like this without the meaningful (content) words:

_____ was very _____. She had _____en _____'s
_____. She didn't _____ a _____ for him. So she
_____ed to _____ a _____ _____ for him.

The words that are left are function words and pronouns. None of them represent meaning in themselves, but because they set up the meaningful parts, they provide subtle meaning cues even in the absence of content words. These pattern markers are used by listeners and readers to make predictions and inferences about what's coming in the text, and to assign sentence patterns to the text they're constructing.

A second system of word markings consists of affixes and internal changes in the words, a system used more often in some other languages than in English. We do, however, use such things as:

➤ tense markers for verbs (*s, ed, ing, en*);

➤ plural and possessive markers for nouns (*s, 's, s'*);

➤ different cases for subject, object and possessive forms of pronouns (*I, me, my, mine; he, him, his*).

Unlike some other languages that use different forms of a noun depending on its case, English uses only its position in the pattern to tell the listener or reader its function. Because we don't need a lot of cues to assign sentence patterns, the language in a text is sometimes redundant. Consider this sentence: *The boys are eating their sandwiches now.* Four cues all mark the plurality: the <s> on boys, the *are* form of *be,* the plural possessive pronoun *their,* and the <s> on *sandwiches.* Redundancy is one way language makes up for ambiguity; it provides extra cues to the same information.

On the other hand, for negatives, for example, we receive only minimal cues. An English clergyman was able to convince language authorities that double (actually multiple) negatives are bad. So we're supposed to say, "I don't have any paper" or "I have no paper" but not "I don't have no paper" — but then how can we make sure our negative is understood? Because of contractions, the negative is often even further reduced: "I can go" and "I can't go" differ only slightly. In some dialects the /t/ disappears and the difference is in the vowels: the positive form (*can*) has a schwa, while the negative (*can't*) has a full vowel because the stress is heavier.

The fact is, we're so good at constructing meaning as listeners and readers that we don't need many cues. As long as we find the text comprehensible, we select from the available cues to make predictions and inferences and we use subsequent cues to confirm or disconfirm our decisions. Authentic, grammatical and meaningful texts are rarely completely ambiguous. When they are, it's likely that the author wasn't aware of the ambiguity because he or she knew what he or she intended to say.

Rules

As we learn to speak a language, we learn its grammar rules. Since those rules aren't "visible" in language, we can't learn them by imitation. So we invent them and then, to be better understood, keep moving toward the conventional rules of our family and community. Kids are pretty good grammarians by the time they start learning to read.

Readers' miscues show that their rules may not be those the author used in producing the text. In this reading, Angela, the African-American fourth-grader we met earlier reading *The Little Brown Hen*, produces a miscue that uses optional rules, rules the author could have used without making a difference.

(c)   could
He stopped by the feed bin. \ "If I should find
            . He   . He
the hen, she'll be hungry," he thought(.) so ∧ he set
down his fishin(g) equipment and scooped up
(c)   the
\corn (and) filled his pockets. He put ∧ corn in his
right pocket and (corn) in his left pocket.

In this example Angela has assigned different rules to the text than the author did. She also inserts words that could have been used by the author. In the second line, she replaces "should" with "could." The author's use of subjunctive here, in a thought attributed to a rural boy, is odd. Angela goes to the more likely verb phrase, "if I could," but then corrects herself. In the next line, without changing any words, she rearranges the clauses and sentences, ending a sentence after hungry and making a separate sentence of "he thought so" by moving "so" back from the next sentence and changing its function.

Now the next sentence starts with "He." She omits the "and" after "corn," but then self-corrects when she reads the following word, "filled," a verb. Her insertion of "the" before the next "corn" follows a rule that common nouns usually get a determiner. Because "corn" in this case is a mass noun (we measure it, we don't count it), it can appear without a determiner if it is indefinite, as the author has treated it here. But, as Angela correctly recalls, the corn has already been identified, and by inserting "the" she shifts from indefinite to definite. She's right and the author is wrong! Her omission of "corn" in the second clause is also a slight improvement, because she uses the rule that redundant elements in successive clauses can be deleted.

I offer this analysis of Angela's changes not to impress you with *my* knowledge of English syntax but with *hers*. This young rural African-American child "knows" the rules of English grammar so well that she can not only deal with the author's complex rules, but create new patterns using her own well learned ones. Again I say, *this is knowledge Angela uses all the time in producing language*, not a linguist's knowledge *about* language. You and I are able to use linguistic terminology to talk about what Angela does in using the syntactic rules of English. Her knowledge is powerful and productive, but tacit.

Meaning and pragmatics level

Once more the central premise of this book: *meaning is constructed by the reader in transacting with the text.* But what characteristics of a text make that construction possible? The answer is both simple and complex. The simple answer is that an authentic language text is meaningful. But that's misleading because it implies that the text is full of meaning. It isn't. The meaning is in the writer and the reader.

Then how does the text figure in the reading of it? We could say instead that an authentic text is *comprehensible* — that is, readers can make sense of it, it has meaning potential for its intended audience, it is a complete enough semiotic representation of meaning to make it possible for readers with sufficient relevant knowledge to make meaning from it. But the text not only represents meaning, it is shaped by the meaning. You and I and our language ancestors have socially constructed language to make it possible for us to share meaning. At every level, language is shaped by this need for it to work in social communication. We can make sense of texts, oral or written, if they follow certain conventions that have grown out of our need to share meaning.

In the rest of this chapter I want to talk about how the writer's meaning shapes a comprehensible text. Halliday (1985) helps us to see that there are three kinds of meaning a text must represent simultaneously. He calls these *experiential, interpersonal* and *textual.*

Experiential meaning

The most obvious kind of meaning represents our experiences or the ideas we've developed from them. If I say "My desk is white," my meaning and yours will define what that means. We share experiences of *whiteness* and *deskness,* and you know I'm referring to a desk that I own or at least have the use of. But if I say "I have a beautiful desk," although you know I *view* it as beautiful, you don't know what characteristics of the desk make me think that. Furthermore, as I talk more about my beautiful desk, you'll discover I'm being sarcastic: "I have a beautiful desk. At least I think it is. It disappeared under a mound of work about two years ago."

Interpersonal meaning

People don't use language just to share experiences. They also share their attitudes, feelings and responses to their experiences, and do so at the same time that they share their ideas.

What follows is another section from "The Man Who Kept House," as read by Betsy. (A complete demonstration of Betsy's miscues can be found in Goodman, Watson and Burke, 1987.)

"Poor baby, you must be hungry," said the woodman. "I'll make some porridge for you.

     the   *(c) I'll*

I'll light a fire in the fireplace, \and the

             (c)   *flash*

porridge will be ready \in a few minutes."

Betsy reads "poor baby" the way one might say it to a young child, with just the right intonation to show that she understands the meaning. This phrase has an interpersonal meaning: "I (the baby's father) feel the baby is pitiable." Betsy's intonation shows that she has understood this meaning: the baby is not poor in an ideational sense, but a father is expressing his feelings for his crying baby. "Poor baby" is sometimes used in other contexts as well, as something people say to each other (not to a baby) to express light-hearted sympathy, or perhaps to mock someone's lament.

The substitution of "in a flash" for "in a few minutes" shows her continuing with the interpersonal meaning of this paragraph. She knows that the father is trying to cheer up the baby and uses a more interpersonal, pragmatically appropriate form. The author, on the other hand, has stayed close to an ideational expression. Betsy pauses after her miscue, as if doing a double-take, and then self-corrects. She isn't just recognizing words, she's making sense. But she's also tentative enough to check her predictions against the expected text. And she shows her ability to construct both kinds of meaning.

Textual Meaning

The third kind of meaning may be a bit harder to grasp. Not only grammar but also meaning is represented by the structure of the text. We talked earlier about *a* and *the* as syntactically equivalent. But the difference between the definite noun that *the* introduces and the indefinite noun that *a* introduces is a semantic one. So Betsy's replacing "a" with "the" shows her use of text features to build meaning. If the fireplace is definite, isn't the fire?

Halliday and Hasan (1976) have studied a number of complex ways that texts are made cohesive, one being ellipsis. In this text the author could have omitted the second *I'll*, joining the two clauses that start the same into a single sentence: "I'll make some porridge for you and light a fire . . ." But since he repeated the *I'll*, Betsy predicts a series of sentences and inserts another *I'll* after *fireplace*. When she doesn't find what she expects — a parallel clause after the comma, perhaps "I'll make" or "I'll cook" — she again self-corrects.

Simultaneous meaning systems

The text represents these three kinds of meaning simultaneously. It brings together the experiential, interpersonal and textual meaning into a single cohesive text. The author uses appropriate syntactic structures to represent the textual meaning, and chooses the right words and word forms to express the subtleties of interpersonal and experiential meaning.

Here are the opening paragraphs of the lead story in my morning newspaper several months ago:

> Washington - The United States assigned 54,000 troops to the Persian Gulf and put 15,000 more on standby yesterday to back up a warning to Saddam Hussein that another attack on Kuwait would result in certain defeat.
>
> Moreover, administration officials hinted that if the Iraqi leader repeated his actions of 1990, the United States will not "repeat the mistakes of the past" and let him off the hook. They even suggested that it might not take an actual invasion of Kuwait to trigger a U.S. response. (*Arizona Daily Star*, 10/10/94, p.A-1)

It's common to think that newspaper stories stick to facts and therefore convey primarily experiential meaning. But all three kinds of meaning are well represented here. The writer represents some things explicitly and experientially:

the number of troops, for example. They are *assigned* to the *Persian Gulf* — but is that the body of water or the region? Does *assigned* mean they are there already? On their way? Just getting their orders? Hussein is also called the *Iraqi leader*, to avoid repetition, but the reader has to already know that they are the same person and infer that *his* and *him* also refer to Hussein. The United States is portrayed as if it were a person, when in fact a reader must infer that it was authorities within the United States government who assigned the troops. We must also understand the subject of *put* to be these same authorities.

The choice of some verbs carries a good deal of interpersonal meaning: *officials hinted*. They (the same officials?) also *suggested*. Can you visualize a press briefing in which these unnamed administration officials (we must infer this is the administration of the President of the United States) *hinted* and *suggested* rather than *stated* or *said*? The verb *warn* has been transformed to the noun *warning*. Textual meaning must be teased out of this verb-turned-noun, which is what got *backed up*. Who was warned? By whom? What was the content of the warning? If the warning involves another attack, can we assume there was a prior attack? Was that the one back a few years or has there already been a new attack? In what manner are the troops that have been assigned going to back up the warning? All this is left to the reader to infer. *Certain defeat* is interpersonal as well, representing the view of the warners that the defeat would be certain.

Besides neatly blending these three kinds of meaning, the writer of this news story has used a number of idioms and figures of speech. *The United States* used to represent the government of the United States is a figure of speech called synecdoche. *Put on standby, back up a warning, off the hook, trigger a response* are all metaphors that rely on shared meaning for understanding. For example, since a trigger is part of a gun, the trigger metaphor implies that the response will happen as surely as a gun is fired when its trigger is pulled — that is, an action by Hussein will make the response an automatic one without any additional decisions having to be made. *Off the hook* is a metaphor from fishing. How is Hussein like a fish and how was he let off the hook he was caught on? Readers may know, or be able to guess.

Even the author's decision to start the second paragraph with *moreover* is significant. Halliday says the first element in any structure takes on great importance. So, *moreover* is a cue to the reader that this second paragraph will have an important relationship to the first but will exceed the first in importance. It therefore sets up the reader's expectation.

Judging by this writer's choices, he or she clearly assumes that readers already know that some prior events have created a crisis. Not until four paragraphs later is the US Ambassador to the UN quoted about Hussein's actions that brought on the crisis. The cues in the text leave it to the reader to infer what sort of action, short of invading Kuwait, might trigger an American response and what the nature of the response might be. That's clever writing, since it's likely that the writer doesn't know the answers to those questions.

I don't mean to critique news writing. All I want to demonstrate is how a writer structures a text to accomplish certain purposes: not only to inform the reader but also to influence the reader's beliefs and attitudes, and to take advantage of what the reader already knows and believes. The three kinds of meaning are interwoven, and the rich use of idiom and metaphor draws the reader into the transaction. This writer also exhibits a sense of audience. Decisions have been made about how much needs to be made explicit and how much can be left to the reader to infer. And we can see how active the reader must be in constructing a personal text, syntactic structure and meaning.

Summary

What I've tried to demonstrate in this chapter is that we can make sense of texts because they are structured in such a way that they provide three kinds of information to us, assuming that we bring sufficient linguistic and cognitive knowledge to our transaction with them. As we read, we're busy using the signal system, the wording and grammar, and the three kinds of meaning representation.

Margaret Meek (1988) points out another thing we've learned from miscue research: the ways texts are constructed not only make them comprehensible but actually teach us to read by reading them. Our search for meaning provides us with the need to and opportunities to develop the necessary strategies for making sense of texts — as we make sense of specific texts, we develop *efficiency* and *effectiveness* in making sense of them. If the texts we read are authentic and we want to make sense of them, we learn to read by reading.

7

*Readers
have an active
brain that they actively
use to make sense
of text.*

The reading process: cycles and strategies

We saw in the preceding chapter how authentic English texts are organized at three basic levels: the graphophonic, the lexico-grammatical and the semantic-pragmatic. We also learned that readers transact with the text to make their own sense of it, and that they use information from all three levels simultaneously to do so. In this chapter we're going to get quite scientific in looking at how the process works, how readers use all this information to make sense.

To do that, we're going to get into the head of the reader. Behaviorists used to tell us that all we could do was observe stimulus and response, because the head is a "black box" we can't see into. But I've always considered that view literally a "no-brainer." In this chapter, as in the whole book, we'll make the assumption that readers have an active brain that they actively use to make sense of written language. We'll examine what goes on in those intelligent heads, remembering that, although we'll look at particular readers of particular texts, we all exist in a culture and society and, therefore, language is always both personal and social.

The construction of meaning

My statement that reading is constructive goes beyond the construction of meaning. The author crafts a text, and in the previous chapter I focussed on the nature of that text and how it works. But it isn't *that* text that the reader is making sense of. The reader constructs *his or her own text*, parallel to the published text, while transacting with it.

During the transaction, the author's text is transformed into the text the reader makes sense of — my miscue research has provided abundant evidence of that. In a study of pronoun miscues, for example, I was able to show that when readers encounter pronouns, they don't "just know" what the pronoun refers to; they *assign* their own referent and then use the appropriate pronoun in their oral reading to match the referent in the text they are constructing. So the types of pronoun miscues readers produce are limited: substitution of other pronouns, a shift to *the*, and a small number of others.

The reader's text is located only in the reader's head! The reading process focusses on this parallel, personally constructed reader text; perception is governed by, and syntax is assigned on the basis of, *that* text. Both structure and meaning are constructed by the reader, and if something goes wrong, then the text in the reader's head must be reconstructed to be sensible. Reader miscues and self-corrections exhibit this process of construction and reconstruction. Readers are striving to understand what the author is trying to say, but the meaning they are building is their own.

A few key ideas can serve as schemas to guide us as we probe the subtleties of this constructive reading process:

➤ Reading is an active process in which readers use powerful strategies in their pursuit of meaning.

➤ Everything readers do is part of their attempt to make sense.

➤ Readers become highly efficient in using just enough of the available information to accomplish their purpose of making sense.

➤ What readers bring to any act of reading is as important for successful reading as anything they use from the published text.

Effective and efficient reading

In a sense, I'm presenting a model of proficient reading. But through my examples of the miscues of developing readers, you've already seen that this model also applies to readers who are far less than fully proficient. There's only one way to make sense of print; proficient readers do it well, less proficient readers not as well, not as efficiently and effectively. So what is proficient reading?

> Proficient reading is both *effective* and *efficient*. It's *effective* in that the reader is able to make sense; it's *efficient* in that this is accomplished with the least amount of time, effort and energy. An *efficient* reader uses only enough information from the published text to be *effective*.

Nothing in this definition says that the sense all readers make of any given text will be the same. No matter how proficient, a reader's comprehension is always dependent on what he or she brings to the reading in terms of knowledge, experience, interest and values. I'm not saying that anything goes. The meanings constructed by proficient readers will always relate to the published text, but they'll be highly personal at the same time. There is a transaction between the reader and the published text and, through it, with the writer. Both writers and readers strive to understand and be understood. How well they succeed depends on what each brings to the transaction and how well they use the process.

Efficient reading tends to be relatively fast. In fact, most of us read (make sense of print) much faster than we listen (make sense of speech), for the simple reason that we can comprehend speech only at the rate it's presented to us, while in reading we choose our own speed. And even average readers read much more rapidly than they listen. Speed is a result of efficiency, not a cause.

Efficiency also produces what some people call fluency. Those who believe comprehension depends on rapid, accurate word recognition define fluency as exactly that. But reading that requires accurate word recognition is very *inefficient*, since it limits the use of cues to identifying words and distracts us from the necessary focus on meaning — in other words, it's *ineffective*. We can read fast precisely because we don't have to recognize every word.

It is certainly true that proficient readers, in general, read more smoothly and with fewer overt miscues than less proficient readers. But again, that's the result of and not a prerequisite for their proficiency.

The cyclical process

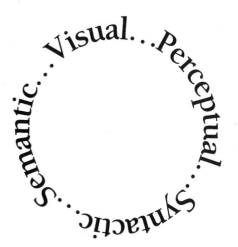

To get from the visual input our eyes provide to our brains to the meaning our brains construct, we must go through four cycles: visual, perceptual, syntactic and semantic. It helps to think of this as a continuous process in which, once we begin to read (receive the visual input), each cycle follows the preceding one. The situational context in which we begin reading immediately sets up meaning expectations that influence what we're looking for when we look at the print.

There's another point to keep in mind: we make leaps. Since our goal in reading is always the construction of meaning, and since we supply much of the information necessary to make our own sense of the text, we can and do leap ahead of the cyclical process. We're such good guessers that we've barely formed a perceptual image before we've decided what the meaning is. Then we fill out the process: we believe we see the letters, know the words, recognize the sentence patterns. Remember your experience with "The Boat in the Basement" (p.38). You were so confident of the meaning that you were sure you saw words and letters that in fact you only thought you saw.

It's true that we use visual information to form perceptions, assign syntax and wording on the basis of our perceptions, and can get to meaning only after we've decided on the language structures and wording we're dealing with. But reading isn't a linear process — we have all kinds of information available all the time. And the information is sufficiently ambiguous that we are constantly leaping to conclusions while, at the same time, being tentative enough to look out for conflicting information.

As I keep reminding you, the brain is the organ of human information processing. In reading, as in everything else, we have a brain in our head and we use it.

The visual cycle

The eye, as we all know, is an optical instrument. It has a lens, with a focal point, and light passing through that lens activates sensors that transport impulses to the brain, which in turn forms perceptions. As light passes through a lens, the rays are reversed so that images appear upside down. We have no sense of this, however, because our brain turns things back upright for us. What we see is less important than what we believe we see.

In reading, light bounces off a page of print to our eyes. Many factors influence the visual cycle in reading: the quality of our eyes, the size of print, light intensity, even our expectation of what we'll see. Over the years my glasses have become increasingly stronger as I've needed more help to cope with small print. But, as perceptual psychologist Paul Kolers (1969) says, "reading is only incidentally visual." What we do with visual input is more important than the quality of the input itself.

Focus and fixation

When the eye moves, it provides only blurred input. In order to provide clear visual input to the brain, it must fix on a point and focus. If we could draw a line from our nose to the page as we read, only a small circle of print would be in clear focus at each fixation, with a much larger fuzzy area of peripheral vision around this clear area. We have a sense of what's there — we certainly see movement peripherally — but it's not clear enough to provide reliable information. I've superimposed on this paragraph a representation of how your visual field might work on a specific fixation. The oval is flattened out because your brain knows that, since the print is arranged in lines, information to the left and right will be more useful than that above and below.

If reading could make use of nothing but exact information, we'd be able to use only what's in sharp focus. But our set for ambiguity makes it possible to use the fuzzy input in the peripheral field as well, because we construct our perceptions on the basis of our expectations. Evidence from miscue research shows how this works.

down

Andrew's eyes dropped ∧, then closed. I went on reading,

and when I looked *down* again, Andrew was asleep.

We did the same and the *horses* broke into a trot.

Horse

Neither Running Bird nor I knew how to ride a

In these examples, the readers incorporated words from their peripheral visual field into their reading of the text. The first shows an insertion miscue (*down* is inserted after *dropped*), the second a substitution (*Running Bird* becomes *Running Horse*). These words aren't just randomly popped in. In most cases, insertions or substitutions from the peripheral field are appropriate to the context, indicating that even input from peripheral vision is used to construct a text that fits the reader's expectations.

Fixations have been studied through eye movement research. One interesting finding is that a reader's first fixation isn't usually at the beginning of a line. That's efficient if the reader has already made a strong prediction about what will be there. If the first fixation confirms the expectation, the reader simply moves on. If not, the eyes regress left to fixate at the beginning of the line.

Distinctive features

In studying phonology, linguists talk about *distinctive features*, key characteristics that distinguish one phoneme from another. But, as we noted, the nature of these distinctive features varies in different contexts. The same is true of the distinctive physical features that distinguish *letters* and *spelling patterns*. The difference between **A** and **H** is that the sides meet in the former and stay parallel in the latter, and the cross bar is a bit lower in the former. But these letters in other fonts have different distinctive features. What we see must be assigned value by our brains as we form perceptions. The brain makes one an <a> and the other an <h> in the contexts in which they are found. Here's another example: **10** could be the numeral form of ten, but in the font I chose it's actually the beginning of **loss**. Our brain continually has to deal with this kind of variability and ambiguity in the features it uses from visual input to form perceptions.

Summarizing the visual cycle

➤ Our eyes scan print from left to right, stopping to fixate at points along the lines.

➤ At each fixation, visual input is sent to the brain by the eye; some is in sharp focus, but more is fuzzy.

➤ What we know about the text structure and meaning causes us to predict what we will see. (Because the brain has this advance information about what it expects the eye to see, the points of fixation are therefore "informed.")

➤ Our knowledge of English orthography, fonts, etc. helps us to know what forms the features we're looking for will take, and to adjust our expectations in advance of seeing them.

➤ Visual input is turned into perceptual images almost instantly.

➤ At key times, the brain may send the eyes scanning back in the text to get more visual input, but most often visual regressions come only at those points where the reader realizes a miscue has disrupted the process of making sense.

The perceptual cycle

Efficient reading uses the least amount of visual information necessary to get to the sense of the text.

I've been arguing in this book that *perception* and not *recognition* is the key process involved in making sense in reading. After visual input, the brain has a very short time to form a perceptual image, and then a very short time to assign value to the image — that is, to guess what is being seen. Speed is an urgent necessity. Imagine that a TV screen is receiving images rapidly and continuously but that those images are disappearing very slowly. That's what happened with early television and computer displays, and as the images piled up, they interfered with the viewers' perception of the whole.

The same for reading. Our brains have to make quick use of what's coming in, because new images keep coming and coming and coming. Predicting what we will see makes immediate perception possible. And here's a crucial point to understand: *what we perceive is based on what we see, but what we see is also based on what we perceive.* It was one of the major lessons you learned in reading "The Boat in the Basement."

A perceptual experiment

Cover the lines below NOW *without looking at them*. Then expose one line at a time, view it for a fraction of a second, and cover it up again. After you look at each line, take a pencil and write down everything you remember seeing.

1. ✪✳✛☙%©®$ƒΦ𝑓∞
2. 149162536496481
3. G N U p V f a z H j l c a
4. Transpotation
5. You're a good reader

If you cheated, or just couldn't avoid looking ahead, try this on an unsuspecting colleague or family member. Expose each line one at a time, only for an instant, and see what they remember and write down. Here are some things you (or they) might have noticed:

➤ You were thrown by the first line because each character, though possibly recognizable in itself, is not part of a system that you easily recognize. You needed much more detail to form an image, so you couldn't remember them.

➤ You knew virtually instantly that line two consists of a series of numerals. Math folks may have been able to write down the whole line, because there is a pattern: 1, 4, 9, 16, etc., the first nine squares. If you did, you had the sense that you'd seen all the numerals instantly. If not, chances are you could only remember somewhere between three and seven of them.

➤ From the third line you were able to write down about the same number of letters, starting from the left side since, as a reader of English, you read from left to right. Readers of Hebrew or Arabic start on the right.

➤ You noticed that line four is almost but not quite a word.

➤ You had a sense of instant comprehension on line five. But did you put a period at the end? The line doesn't have one!

By the way, were the 4s you wrote in the second line closed like the one in the book or open like this: ⊔? You probably wrote not what you saw, but what you perceived, and what you perceived was what you expected once you knew you were looking at numerals. Your set for ambiguity supported your perception. You used the features of the 4 you saw, but within your expectation that it was a numeral, you used your numeral schema to assign it to the four numeral and wrote the example of "fourness" you normally produce. In reading, perception is an intelligent process in which you give values to the features of what you see in the context of trying to make sense of print. See how smart you are as a reader?

Now let me ask, did you write the numerals and dots to the left of the lines? Most people aren't even aware that the lines are numbered; their brain treats those numerals as outside the significant display. Did you number yours? Did you not number even though you were aware of the numbering? Or did you only now realize that the lines are numbered? As you see, the brain perceives what it does on the basis of what it knows and expects.

Perception is a process of constructing images from visual input by drawing on the schemas we've formed for organizing what we see to fit what we know. The process is always constructive. Our perceptions aren't controlled by what we see. We don't just recognize letters and words by matching what we see to some stored image. We construct perceptions in response to what we see; we select from what we see what will be most useful in forming the perceptual images we need to make sense of what we are seeing.

This small experiment demonstrates an important aspect of efficient reading: the more meaningful a visual display is, the easier it is to read. In the first line you could remember only a few of the characters, but you easily got the meaning of the last meaningful sentence with the same amount of visual input — in other words, you made efficient use of the information available to you to form high-quality perceptions. Remember, efficient reading uses the least amount of visual information necessary to get to the sense of the text.

Summarizing the perceptual cycle

➤ As soon as the eye, controlled by the brain, supplies visual input, we select from it the variant forms of features we expect to see, and give perceptual values to them: in one flash, a half circle and a line is *c l*; in another, it's *d*. If the type font has serifs (lines at the ends of the main strokes of letters, as you see printed here), we expect them and discount them as distinctive features. Sans-serif fonts (without those embellishments) are perceived without any expectation of the appendages. We adjust our expectations when we encounter all caps as well, as seen in most street signs, billboards and other environmental print.

➤ From what we see, we construct perceptual images that make use of our sense of meaning of the text we are reading, as well as its syntactic and semantic structures. We also draw on all of our knowledge of the world.

➤ Because our perceptions are so strongly influenced by our expectations, we may have a strong sense that we saw something different from what we actually saw. But unless we have some problem with making sense of the text, we are unlikely to know that our perceptions don't match reality.

➤ When our brain finds that what is being perceived doesn't fit with what was previously understood and/or expected, we have two options. Most often

we revalue what we have perceived and form an alternative perception —
we literally "change our minds" about what we've seen. But we can also
send the eye regressing back in the text for more input to form another
image.

The syntactic cycle

*Readers construct the syntax
of the text as they are
constructing the
meaning.*

In the third cycle of reading, which I've
always called the *syntactic* cycle, the reader
must immediately treat perceptual images
as language: sentence patterns must be
assigned and, through them, meaning. You
had that confirmed in the previous experiment as you easily assigned a sentence
structure to the last line. Over time, I've broadened my understanding of what is
involved in this middle level of language; I feel now that *lexico-grammatical* is a
more correct term for this cycle, since it includes the assignment of wording to
the text. I'm keeping *syntactic* here, however, to emphasize that, unless the reader
can deal with the text as structured language, comprehension is impossible.
That's one important reason why the view of reading as word recognition is not
acceptable: it can't explain that the meaning of a text is far more than the sum of
the meanings of the words.

By the way, although I'm borrowing from both Chomsky and Halliday in
this explanation of the lexico-grammatical cycle, as I often do, please don't hold
either responsible for my application of their insights and concepts.

Constructing grammar while constructing meaning

Speakers and writers use their knowledge of the structure (grammar) of the
language to produce comprehensible texts. As listeners and readers make sense
of those texts, they also make language of them. But unlike graphophonic
signals, grammar is not directly observable. The reader must bring to their
reading a knowledge of the grammar of the language and *assign* grammar to the
text using cues the speaker or writer has built in.

When I say grammar is not directly observable, I mean that there are no
"N"s or "V"s or "SVO"s tagged onto each word or sentence, and no tree-diagram
is visible in the printed text. The author has used grammar, but the reader must
construct his or her own grammatical structure in making sense of it. At the
beginning of each clause or sentence, you must predict what you think it's
structure will be and then process what follows within the structure you assign.
If your first prediction doesn't work out, you may have to reconsider or reread
(or ask the speaker to repeat). Fortunately, your inferences usually lead to
efficient predictions because you know the language so well.

"Grammar" is not a phenomenon unique to language, although it's usually a language word. The world is a structured, patterned place. We expect it to make sense. But the order or structure is not often explicit, and our brains build hypotheses to test against the reality of the world. For example, public places usually have separate sanitary facilities for men and for women. (Are they *toilets, restrooms, bathrooms, lavatories, gents and ladies* or what in the polite speech of your dialect and community?) If you're looking for *Women* and find one marked *Men*, you can usually assume the other is opposite, beside, across an aisle, etc. However, in my university's College of Education, someone (a committee?) decided to put women's facilities on odd floors, men's on even. That arrangement is so unpredictable that newcomers often search frantically and uncomfortably, trying every variant of the symmetry they've learned to assume. They can't believe the appropriate facility isn't in one of the predictable locations.

Assigning structure

Readers use cues in the text to assign a surface syntactic structure and then a deep structure. In Halliday's sense, they assign functions to components of structures at one language level that have functions in larger structures at the level above. The levels are constructed simultaneously since, even as they begin to read a sentence, readers must have a grammatical frame for selecting from visual input and forming perceptions. If they find input that can't fit their grammatical frames, they'll either try another structure or regress, get more information and then assign a different syntactic pattern.

Readers expect language to have a syntactic structure that follows the rules and other schemas they already control. Neither the surface structure nor the underlying deep structure is apparent, but to construct both, readers use their knowledge of transformational grammatical rules. Since they predict where the text is going, they have to watch for cues that confirm or disconfirm their prediction. Here's a miscue that shows the reader's prediction of a different pattern than the one the author used:

Umi was able to make his way to the stockade∧
Around   *he*
around the building(.) He climbed . . .

Pablo, a fourth-grade reader, decides that the first sentence ends at the end of the line. It seems unlikely at this level, but perhaps he is still influenced by early experiences with one of the primary basal readers which, in using only single-line sentences, lead children to expect sentences to end where the line does. In this case, ending after "stockade" produces a grammatical and comprehensible sentence, but now Pablo has a second prepositional phrase left over: "around the building."

If he couldn't figure out what to do with the extra phrase, he'd probably disconfirm his prediction, look back in the text to find where he'd gone wrong and self-correct, or at least try to. (Our research shows that about one-third of miscues are self-corrected, and a higher percentage of syntactically unacceptable miscues are corrected than those that produce acceptable sentence patterns.) But by starting a new sentence with the leftover phrase and omitting the sentence-ending period in the middle of the line, Pablo creates a new syntactically acceptable pattern. What makes it possible is that *around the building* is an adverbial phrase, so it can occur in different positions. The meaning isn't the same, of course, but the difference is minor.

Intonation in oral texts

Oral reading shows the sentence pattern the reader has assigned.

Since this reader decides what sentence pattern to assign when he makes a miscue, we know, theoretically, that he must also be doing so when there's no miscue and his sentence patterns match the author's — there is simply no other way for readers (or listeners) to get to the grammar and through it to the meaning except to construct it themselves. Reading would be far too inefficient if readers had to correctly "identify" every word, letter and punctuation mark before making decisions about the grammar and meaning of what they are reading.

Besides, Pablo's intonation confirms that he is assigning syntactic patterns as he reads. When he starts the sentence, his intonation is one used for statements. We know he's ended the sentence after *stockade* because his voice produces the "fade-fall" pattern common at the ends of many English statements. When he starts reading *Around*, as listeners we know that he's begun a new statement. Questions and commands have quite different intonation patterns than statements.

Intonation in any oral language is the overall pattern of stress, pitch and pause patterns that modulates the sound sequences. We don't speak in monotones. Speech is rhythmic, rising and falling, fading and flaring as it bops along to its meter and tune. We more easily hear this musical characteristic in other people's languages: Chinese sounds "sing-song" to an English-tuned ear because it uses tone differences more than English does. German is often described as "guttural," French as "lyric."

As a listener, you use intonation to cue you to the sentence patterns that are coming. You predict by how utterances start, and you use the fade-fall pattern at the end to confirm that the structure you predicted is working. To me, one of the wonders of language is that, although linguists have enormous difficulty in describing the complexity of intonation, even young children master it with ease.

Halliday (1977) found that Nigel, a toddler, used two different intonation patterns very early in his language development, one to comment on the world, the other to ask for information or make demands. Depending on the intonation, "Mommy shoes" could mean "Those are Mommy's shoes" or "Give me (I want) Mommy's shoes."

In our own research, we almost always had a sense of the sentence patterns the reader was constructing, even if non-words were included. Frequently we could even tell from the intonation what part of speech the non-words had for that reader.

But intonation isn't a characteristic of individual words or word parts. It's a contour for the whole pattern of oral language, a characteristic of oral language as a whole — "supersegmental," in linguist terms. It has no counterpart in written language. Although punctuation helps the reader to organize the sentence patterns, it does so in a more minor way. And punctuation occurs at a point rather than as a contour.

In Pablo's case, the period comes much too late to help him make his decision about the sentence pattern; he's already decided where the text is going. It's just a tiny bit of information, and he doesn't perceive it because he doesn't expect it to be there. Of course, if he had disconfirmed his prediction, if something had gone wrong in his construction of sentence patterns and meaning, he might have noticed the period when he regressed for more cues.

Assigning wording

In speaking, while we are assigning the syntactic structure, just before we produce an utterance, we also choose the words and their forms. We know that must be so because, as the clauses come together in the deep structure and the surface structure is generated, several decisions are required that affect which words are needed and which forms of them will be used. In an earlier example (see p.82), application of a cohesion rule resulted in deleting the *you'll have to* from the last three clauses. Past tense verbs must take past tense forms, plural nouns take plural forms. Pronouns must be chosen appropriately for the situation. The wife addresses her husband as *you*; in his response he says *I*.

Wording is assigned the way syntax is assigned, and each helps to determine the other. The choice of a particular word or idiom may cause changes in the surface syntactic structure. In writing a note, Mr. C., an aphasic adult, knew he would have trouble writing the word *instructions*, so he wrote *user's manual* instead. To do so, he had to use a different structure, not just different wording.

Does the reader mirror the writer's process, starting with the words that are there on the page? My answer is "No, but . . ." The reader is intent on making sense. To deal with the text, the reader assigns the syntactic structure as each sentence begins, or even before. He or she also assigns the *expected* wording before words are actually encountered. That doesn't mean that the reader isn't paying attention to the words in the text, but that there's a tension between the reader's expectations and the text wording.

When you read "The Boat in the Basement" you demonstrated how the strengths of your predictions could cause you to miss aberrations in the text, because you had already decided what would be there. Readers are constructing meaning and constructing the text, including its structure, as they read. They are constructing the wording, too. They don't do this without considering the wording of the published text, but they are not controlled by that wording.

Here is another example from "The Man Who Kept House":

day
So the next morning the wife
went off to the forest. The
husband stayed home and
job
began his wife's work.

The reader produces meaning with her own words that fit the context: that is, she makes sense of the text but predicts words that are different from the author's. In using "day" for "morning" and "job" for "work," she preserves the experiential meaning. She doesn't think "day" is spelled m-o-r-n-i-n-g, but gets the idea and uses another word to express it. Her choice of "job" probably indicates that that's the word she'd use in talking about what people do. Neither word changes the meaning of the text, so there's no reason for her to correct. The purpose of reading is to make sense, not to get the words right.

I said that assigning wording and syntax comes last in speaking and writing, but I should add that how the words are pronounced and spelled comes last in the wording. In speaking, the syntax will determine the intonation and that, in turn, will determine stress and pronunciation of words. In writing, most individual words have standard spellings and, if we know them, they supersede any rules we might use to invent spellings.

Words and context

Let's take time out to clear up another common misunderstanding about reading that arises out of the word-centered view of language. Even advocates of that view concede that context has some affect on the likelihood that readers will be able to read a particular word. But they treat context as one of several cues *to* word identification or recognition, and that has things upside down. The reality is that in the process of making sense of print, *we* decide what the words are, using not only their graphophonic characteristics (what they look and might sound like), but also a full set of syntactic cues and a full semantic setting.

In oral reading, we might produce a word that matches the expected response to the text, and we might not. Effective readers usually read the words we expect them to read, but they also substitute synonyms or words that make sense but aren't exact matches. They sometimes produce non-words, or real words that change the meaning to some degree. There's a context for every word (the grammar and meaning of the sentence and the text), but the reader uses more than that for deciding on the wording of the text.

The reader is primarily concerned with making sense of everything. Sometimes that means keeping both the sense and the grammar but changing the wording; sometimes it means keeping the syntax but producing non-words. Most often in successful reading, the wording and grammar are the same as in the original text because readers control the process so well, not because they are accurately identifying words. Getting the words right is a by-product of making sense of the whole and not the other way around.

In a study of second-, fourth- and sixth-grade readers, across populations, grades and proficiencies, 60% of all miscues were syntactically acceptable before self-correction. The readers used the grammatical information effectively even if they lost some meaning and changed the wording. Less than 20% of all miscues resulted in losing the deep structure entirely, even among second-grade readers. For all groups in the study, 60-80% of the word substitution miscues had the same grammatical function as the expected response: noun for noun, verb for verb, preposition for preposition, etc. We could even tell the grammatical function of many non-word substitutions from the reader's intonation and retention of the grammatical word endings: *$pousts/posts, $beering/bearing.*

Often words are inserted or omitted in reading without producing syntactically unacceptable sentences. The following examples are from a Spanish-speaking fourth-grader reading from "Sancho, the Homesick Steer."

        the

She poured warm milk into a bottle,

    she

then ∧ sat on the floor with the

calf's head in her lap.

    the

"So ∧ young (to) lose your mother,

my Sancho. . ."

This reader makes the "bottle" definite by switching from "a" to "the." She inserts "she" in the next clause, showing that she has inferred the omitted subject. Her insertion of "the" before "young" in the next excerpt shows a similar inference. The author has omitted "you are" in the dialog ("you are so young to lose your mother") to create a conversational tone. The reader turns "young," an adjective, into a noun by putting "the" in front of it and then turns "to lose," an infinitive, into a transitive verb by omitting "to." She is constructing an alternate grammar as she strives to make sense, to construct meaning. By the way, this child giggled as she read "Sancho," the calf's name. "That's what we call a married lady's boyfriend in this part of Texas," she said. Kids just can't help imposing their knowledge on what they read.

A sixth-grade Arabic immigrant produced the following:

that

I thought ∧ the (re)frigerator would explode.

He inserted "that," an optional element the author could have used to introduce the clause in this grammatical structure. By inserting it here the reader shows his control of the sentence structure of English, a language he's still learning. If he didn't control English syntax, he couldn't have produced this miscue. In the same sentence the child says "frigerator" for "refrigerator." That could reflect his second-language background but more likely it's simply the immature form used by many kids who are native speakers of English.

When we read we make sense of texts. One characteristic of texts is that they have wording, and we use the wording in making sense. But the wording we produce when we read is one we have assigned to the text, based on the meaning we've constructed. We don't use context to identify words. We assign wording, in context, as we make sense.

Summarizing the syntactic cycle

➤ This cycle starts with employing the perceptual images to assign a surface structure that will serve as a structural schema for what we expect in the text. As we begin a sentence, we must decide whether it will be question, command or statement.

➤ From this surface structure, we assign a deep structure that makes it possible for us to unpack the clauses to get to meaning and to construct meaning from the ways the clauses relate to each other.

➤ Then we generate a new surface structure and wording, which may or may not match that of the text. Often our syntactic predictions are so strong that we miscue on cues in the text, particularly on punctuation. We may "read through" terminal punctuation, using a prepositional phrase to complete a predicted pattern. Several readers produced the same miscue on this sentence: *He heard a faint tapping and a voice calling, somewhere above.* Some readers read it as: *He heard a faint tapping and a voice calling, "somewhere above."* In this case, the wording stays the same although the syntactic structure and the meaning are changed, but it's possible that as a surface structure is regenerated the wording is also changed. Several earlier examples show such changes.

➤ If the syntactic patterns and wording the reader generates cause no problems in constructing meaning, there is no reason for readers to reprocess or regress. On the other hand, if the assigned syntax or wording doesn't work out, the reader is likely to try alternatives or to regress to get more input.

The semantic cycle

Our brain shifts from processing language to processing meaning.

As we assign a syntactic structure to the text we're reading, we get to the underlying structure, unpack the clauses and arrive at meaning — that is, the meaning cycle flows from the syntactic/lexico-grammatical cycle. It's at this transition that our brain shifts from processing language to processing meaning. I'm utterly confident in saying that, and the subjects we've looked at through their miscues have surely made such a shift.

But I don't know how it happens. Some people believe that the brain has a language, probably biochemical, to which it moves as it deals with meaning. In any case, it's useful to think of reading (and all language processes in use) as *psycholinguistic* — that is, involving both thought and language. I also find it useful to think of thought as separable from language.

But let me again stress what I've already said in many ways: *without meaning, there is nothing in language*. The entire process of reading integrates around our determination to make sense of what we're reading. Although I call this fourth and last cycle *semantic* — the one in which meaning is constructed — I couldn't discuss the visual, perceptual and syntactic cycles without referring to meaning. So focussed is reading on making sense that the visual input, the perceptions we form, and the syntactic patterns we assign are all directed by our meaning construction.

As we saw earlier, we are capable of making sense of something before we have all the information we need, often leaping ahead of each cycle before we've finished using it. We can see the same thing in oral conversations, especially among people who know each other well. For instance, we sometimes find ourselves understanding and responding to what someone is saying before the speaker is finished, and not finishing our own statements when it's obvious the listener has already made sense of what we're saying. Readers who are reading a text in a field they know well sometimes turn pages at an unbelievable clip!

Again I'm using the simple "semantic" designation for this cycle because I'm used to it, when really I should be calling it "semantic-pragmatic," since pragmatic features of the text and of the cultural context of particular literacy events clearly come into play. I'll be dealing with these pragmatic aspects of this cycle of the reading process as well, by discussing a number of key concepts that can help us understand the process.

Given and new information

In any discourse, once new information is introduced it's frequently referred to again and again. (For our purposes, "discourse" is any kind of continuing communication between two or more people — written text is a common form of discourse, even though the writer and reader are not usually in the same place and time.) *New* information and already *given* information are represented very differently. In general, language has ways of referring to given information without repeating it.

In the discourse between husband and wife in the example on page 82, the husband responds: *"I can do all that."* *Do all that* has no meaning out of context, but we know it refers to the list of tasks the wife has just specified. No need to repeat them, since the reader builds a reference to the given information in the text that he or she is constructing. Note that the reader must establish this co-reference; the text only points out that it's given information.

There's a general rule of discourse, which I've come to call "the rule of economy," that requires us to minimize the repetition of information once it's given. For example, once nouns have been introduced we follow up with pronouns, unless their use will result in too much ambiguity for the reader. In comprehending discourse, less is more. Readers are able to infer references when the text signals that information is already given. That makes new information stand out. But it also requires that the reader construct a personal text parallel to the one being read, in which all the implicit connections become explicit to the reader. Without this active construction of text and meaning by the reader, comprehension would be impossible.

Meaning as input and as output

The ability to make sense of what we read is always limited by how much we already know about what we are reading. No text can ever be so cleverly composed that all literate readers can make sense of it. And not even the most effective and efficient reader can make sense of everything ever written. When we construct meaning from reading, we must draw on what we know, what we believe and what we value. Here are two logical corollaries of these statements:

➤ The more we know about what we're reading, the easier it will be to read.

➤ What a reader knows and believes will strongly influence the meaning he or she constructs.

The meaning we bring to the reading is available to us in every cycle, but it's particularly influential as we move from our sense of the syntactic patterns to the semantic structures. Our inferences and predictions will be shaped by our semantic expectations and the schemas we use to organize the meaning we are constructing.

If writers want to be comprehensible, they must write with a sense of the experience, cognitive schema and beliefs of their target audience, and provide examples and other opportunities for the readers to build meaning on what they already know. I repeat yet again, reading is a transaction. The text has a meaning potential but readers change the text by what they bring to it, and change themselves by adding to or changing what they know as they read.

Assimilation and accommodation

Sometimes new information fits neatly into what we already know. But sometimes it doesn't fit at all, and may even conflict with our basic understandings and beliefs. Then we must either reject it or change some of our schemas. In his work on the construction of meaning, Piaget differentiated between these two kinds of meaning construction and learning: what he called *assimilation* and *accommodation* (Piaget and Imhelder, 1969). In our research we found many examples of both.

Uncorrected high-quality miscues, which the reader usually isn't even aware of, are likely to indicate assimilation. Accommodation of information is a more difficult part of the learning process, however, and miscues that show problems with accommodation may reflect what Piaget called "disequilibrium."

In a story about a boy who gets in trouble because of his tinkering, this line occurs: *Freddie hurried to his cellar worktable.* Of 32 young research subjects who read this, 13 substituted *the* for *his*, although nothing like this happened for the other occurrences of *his* in the same story. These readers clearly could not accommodate the notion that a boy could have his own worktable. The same story contains this detailed description of Freddie building a flashlight:

> Carefully he taped the batteries end to end on the ruler so that they touched. He tied the wire tight across the bottom of the end battery. Then he ran the wire up the sides of the two batteries to the bulb. After winding the wire around the bottom of the bulb, he taped it in place.

> Next he placed the bulb so that it touched the cap on the top battery. The bulb began to glow! Freddie taped the bulb in place on the ruler. Now he had a homemade flashlight for Elizabeth.

Almost all of our readers could retell this section in considerable detail. It was easy to assimilate the information into their understanding of the text, and so it was easy to remember.

A text is easy or hard for a reader to make sense of depending on whether it is easily assimilated, or whether it requires accommodations in the reader's schemas and understandings. All of us have had an "Aha!" experience while reading: suddenly something we hadn't quite understood is crystal clear. A major accommodation has taken place in our schema for some idea or process, perhaps after great discomfort (disequilibrium) that resulted from a conflict between what we thought we understood and what we were experiencing.

Often, though, we construct a meaning which is more what we knew and believed before the reading than what we learned during it. We either ignore any conflicting information or assimilate it — make it consistent with our schemas, even if it isn't. And it's not just weak readers I'm talking about, or poorly informed ones who misunderstand what they read. Even the most scholarly readers are prone to construct meaning based on their own belief system or paradigm when reading texts that represent different perspectives.

Assimilation is more pleasant when we get support in our reading for what we already know and believe: a story, an example, a terrific idea that doesn't challenge what we know but provides a comfortable, easy extension to it.

As a writer, I hope you've been able to make sense of what I've been saying, whether through assimilation or the more painful accommodation. But I'd be denying my own theory of the constructive nature of reading if I didn't admit to myself that some of you a lot of the time, and a lot of you some of the time, are constructing meaning quite different from what I'm trying to express.

Integration of experiential, interpersonal and textual meaning

You may remember these three terms from my earlier discussion of Halliday's view that three kinds of meaning are represented in texts, interwoven and supporting each other (see pp.86-87). The textual is most closely related to the syntactic cycle, since the text has both a syntactic and a semantic structure. My discussion on given and new information shows how textual meaning is necessary to constructing the experiential and interpersonal meaning.

Sometimes interpersonal meaning is so subtle in a text, particularly in the kind of informational text we find in a textbook or a news magazine article, that we are influenced without being aware. We may treat as factual information what is in fact a cleverly selective treatment of the topic, designed to influence our beliefs and values. Sometimes the interpersonal message is so subtle (in humor or sarcasm, for example) that we miss it altogether.

Pragmatics plays a major role in our ability to construct interpersonal meaning or detect subtleties. We've used a story called "The Clever Turtle" in our miscue research, an African ancestor of Uncle Remus's *Brer Rabbit in the Briarpatch*. A turtle is caught after it has destroyed the village corn field, and the people are trying to decide on a suitable punishment. "Do anything you want to me," the turtle says, "but please don't throw me into the river." Of course the people do just that, and the turtle swims happily away.

Virtually every second-grade child who read for us understood the story line and plot sequence but missed completely the trick the turtle was playing on the people. In Phyllis Hodes' miscue study of Hassidic Jewish children reading in English and Yiddish (their home language), one seven-year-old went right to the trick in his retelling: "If you want somebody to do something, tell them to do the opposite." (Hodes, 1976)

Halliday has helped us to see that all texts represent layered meaning. A really great work of literature, whether for children or adults, will afford pleasure and be comprehensible to a wide range of readers at a wide range of depth and breadth, depending on what they bring to it. Ironically, reading instruction that focusses too much on reading comprehension as an exact reproduction of an invariant experiential meaning may distract young readers from the interpersonal meaning in reading.

Influence of context of situation

Very early in this book, I asked you to think of each act of reading as a literacy event, with a context of situation that frames the reading and gives it authentic purposes and functions. To understand the semantic cycle of reading, we must remember that the meaning a reader is constructing depends on the reader's *purposes*, the *functions* the reading serves for the reader, and the *field*, *tenor* and *mode* of the particular *genre*. The events that precede and follow the literacy event also influence the reader's getting to meaning — think of cramming for an exam, for example.

Comprehending and comprehension

Our miscue research has taught us to differentiate between two related reading phenomena: *comprehending*, which is the process of making sense of written language, and *comprehension*, which is the resulting meaning. In other words, we consider comprehending the process, comprehension the product.

Traditionally, comprehension has received the most attention. Tests have been constructed to measure it, and scores on these tests, combined with tests of reading skills, have been used to judge reading proficiency. This approach is based on the assumption that all readers of comparable proficiency will be equally able to comprehend texts of appropriate difficulty, regardless of content.

That is not a tenable assumption, as must be clear to you by now. Comprehension depends not just on reading proficiency, but also on the knowledge the reader brings to the reading — always. Moreover, the tests are administered after the reading and so focus on what readers can recall from their reading. If the test is a paper-and-pencil test, it reduces comprehension to the knowledge displayed in answers to questions which often are quite superficial.

In our research, we used open-ended retellings instead, asking our research subjects to tell us everything they could remember from the story. When they appeared to have finished, we then asked open-ended questions to encourage them to be more inclusive in their retellings. We found it a useful approach, but it was still limited by the fact that it was a post-reading task.

In miscue analysis, however, we are able to get a measure of comprehending, of the reader's success in the *process* of making sense of the text. We combine two miscue analysis scores to get this measure. The first is the percentage of miscues that are semantically acceptable, where the meaning is successfully constructed. We add to that the percentage of semantically unacceptable miscues that are successfully corrected, and the combined score we call the *comprehending score*. It provides a measure, as the reader is reading, of how well he or she is constructing meaning. Correlations between the comprehending score and the retelling score are moderate, as we expected they would be. Though comprehension depends on comprehending, it also depends on prior knowledge, so the correlation can't be very high.

Summarizing the semantic cycle

➤ In reading, everything comes together around making sense, so we leap toward meaning. We build a meaning for the text as we are moving from visual to perceptual to syntactic structure and wording.

➤ As long as the meaning we are constructing is coherent and consistent with what we have understood from the text up to that point, and with our expectations, we continue to move forward in the text.

➤ When we can't make sense, or when we realize there's been a miscue that has disrupted our sense-making, we have two options: rethink and assign new meaning, new syntax, new wording, new perceptions; or regress to the point where things went wrong.

➤ Regression often takes us to the beginning of a structure, a sentence or a clause. We then use additional visual and perceptual information to assign a new structure and meaning.

➤ If that fails, or if we choose to, we can suspend moving to meaning and read ahead looking for cues that will make the meaning clear. Even as proficient readers, we sometimes become aware that minor aspects of meaning are eluding us. But we're usually content with that as long as we have enough meaning to make continued reading worthwhile.

Psycholinguistic strategies

I've been building the case that, as we read, our minds are actively busy making sense of print, just as they are always actively trying to make sense of the world. Our minds have a repertoire of *strategies* for sense-making. In reading, we can call these *psycholinguistic* because there's continuous interaction between thought and language.

We start with the text, written language, and use the cues from the various language levels to construct our own parallel text and meaning. We draw on our sense-making strategies all the time we're reading, but some of the cycles draw on some strategies more than others. All of these strategies have their counterparts in making sense of what we hear (listening), and in making sense of the world.

Initiation/recognition strategies

To read, our minds must make a decision to read, although this may happen so naturally that we're not aware we've deliberately decided. Try this: you're sitting across from someone wearing a print dress. You're aware it has a pattern, but it takes a while to realize that the pattern is actually writing — it says something. Now that you know, you read it easily and wonder what took you so long to recognize it as writing. (I'm talking here about recognizing patterns as written language, not recognizing letters and words. Recognizing written language initiates the reading process in all respects.)

Reading is a deliberate act and we have strategies for deciding there's a text to be read and for initiating the reading process. Only after reading is initiated are the other strategies activated, and we begin to make sense. Obviously we use this set of strategies at the beginning of reading every text, but we also do so after each time we stop, when the font or language changes, and when we change our purpose for reading.

Termination strategies

Starting and stopping are closely related and, like initiation, termination may occur one or more times in the reading of every text. Stopping is as deliberate a decision as starting. It occurs at the end of the text, of course, but not only there. There are many reasons for terminating (in no particular order):

loss of interest	poor lighting
interruption	poorly written
no more time available	incomprehensible
disappointment in the quality	offensive
not what one expected	distractions
purpose satisfied	redundant
illegible	boring

Stopping your reading because you're at the end of a text is actually a relatively rare use of terminating strategies. If you're reading a 1143 page novel, it's unlikely you'll stop only when you are done. But where will you stop? At the end of a chapter or section? Does stopping include marking your place with a bookmark or a turned-down corner? Do you put the book in a special place? I mentioned earlier that newspaper journalists plan their writing knowing that most readers won't finish every article they start. But what makes us decide to stop reading one item and go on to something else? Do we intuitively know we've read as much as we care or need to?

I've made the point that initiating and terminating reading involve strategies because understanding that helps us to put the other strategies in some perspective. Also, knowing how often we stop before the end of a text helps us to accept that young readers have the same need and right.

Sample/selection strategies

Psycholinguist George Miller researched how much information the human mind can gather from a single graphic display (1956). He concluded that we are able to perceive from three to seven bits of information, but what those bits are depends on the schemas our mind imposes on the image of the display our perception produces: letters, shapes, words, phrases or whole sentences. Furthermore, the graphic display is itself ambiguous, as we saw earlier: letters may take many forms and shapes in many contexts, for example. In English, word beginnings, particularly consonants, carry more useful information than the rest of the letters. In any case, what our brain tells the eye to look for depends on what we expect to see.

Sample/selection is one of the key strategies we use. We choose from the display only the most useful information, by drawing on everything we know about the writing system of our language, everything we know about the language, and everything we know about the text and the meaning we have created up to the point of our visual fixation on the print. In other words, *we choose what is most useful on the basis of what we already know.*

This is one of those key insights that contradicts common sense. We're used to thinking that readers read carefully and use as much of the text information as possible. But what we've learned in this book is the opposite: efficient reading uses as little information as necessary to get to the meaning of the text.

If that's right, then we need highly efficient strategies for sampling and selecting to be efficient readers. And the more we already know, the more efficient our strategies will be. People learning to read are not as efficient as they will become, and all of us are less efficient when we read material that's difficult for us to understand because we don't have sufficient background knowledge to deal with the meaning.

Prediction/inference strategies

In discussing the cycles, I made a number of references to the role of expectations in reading. As active readers, we don't wait until we have "all the information" before we "make-up our minds." We are constantly anticipating where a text is going, what will come next, what we will see, what structures we will encounter, and we make inferences from what we think we've seen and predicted. Our predictions are based on the information we've selected and sampled from the text, but they also guide the process of selecting and sampling.

A *prediction* is an anticipation of what will come in the text. An *inference* is additional information the reader supplies. Inferences are possible and necessary because no text is a complete representation of the meaning. Often, what we infer is later made explicit in the text and that confirms our inference, but as we read we don't differentiate between what we know because it's explicit and what we know because we're able to make strong inferences. Our predictions are based on our inferences and our inferences are based on our predictions. All the strategies work to support each other.

All of us find it easier to read texts that deal with things we know a lot about. We all know, too, that texts that look easy can be hard if we don't bring much meaning or interest to them, that the more predictable a text is for us, the easier it will be for us to make sense. Since the role of predicting in reading has become recognized, a whole new genre of books for young children has come to the fore: *predictable books* that contain strong, easy-to-predict patterns.

In 1967, I summarized what I knew then about the reading process by calling it a *psycholinguistic guessing game* to emphasize the role of prediction and inference in proficient reading. Now I understand that our ability to make sense of what is always ambiguous is what makes all language, all human communication, possible. We *make* language make sense. We sample just enough, select only the most useful cues. We use all we know, our schemas, to infer what we don't know and predict what is to come.

Confirmation/disconfirmation strategies

In all this we need to maintain a proper balance between confidence and caution. We need to be confident when we're making sense or moving toward it, and cautious that our "psycholinguistic guesses" are supported as we read further. This tentativeness is a characteristic of reading: we take risks but we stay alert for contradiction.

As a result of our need to be tentative, we use a set of confirming and disconfirming strategies. You met those strategies when you examined your own reading and in the samples of children's reading we've looked at through this book. Readers' oral miscues reflect sample/selection and prediction/inference strategies, and we spotted the tentativeness that caused readers to pause, regress, change their minds, and correct when necessary and possible. Readers confirm and continue, or disconfirm and reprocess to see where things went wrong and get back to meaning.

Confirming or disconfirming results from encountering information that supports or conflicts with predictions and inferences. Disconfirming leads to gathering more information by either rethinking the perceptual images or by actually regressing in the text to sample again and select more information that will lead to new predictions and new inferences — changes in the meaning, ultimately. And if readers still can't make sense of the text, they can either read ahead and hope that new information will help them resolve the lack of comprehension, or stop reading (terminate).

Correction strategies

Miscue research and the research of Marie Clay (1968) reveal that correcting is one of the most important bits of evidence that readers are intent on comprehending. Readers correct when they have disconfirmed their predictions and inferences, often immediately. When they produce partial miscues, they may correct even before they've fully said what they were thinking. These instant corrections seem to reflect a reprocessing of information: tentative readers literally change their minds about what they've read.

But often readers continue to read long past a miscue, come to a point of disconfirming — that is, realize that there is a conflict between what they expected and what they encountered — and then search back through the text, usually silently. This process may involve a long pause, perhaps as much as 30 seconds.

Not all miscues need to be corrected. Our research shows that the average rate of correction for most readers is less than one-third. Many miscues show that readers construct a meaningful text even if it differs in minor or major ways from the published text. But miscues that show a loss of meaning or disruption to the meaning-making process need correction. Those are the moments we find readers attempting to correct their miscues, and usually succeeding. As I said, sometimes the corrections are so immediate that the reader doesn't even finish saying a word. In other cases, the miscues follow a word and may reflect a change just in that word or its intonation. Sometimes the regression takes the reader back to the beginning of a clause or sentence.

Readers who correct miscues that don't need to be corrected are *inefficient*: they distract themselves from the central task of making sense by their preoccupation with accuracy. Readers who persistently fail to correct when they need to do so are likely to be *ineffective*: they lose a lot of the meaning.

I need to emphasize that the correction of miscues in oral reading needs to be *self*-correction. Only readers who decide for themselves when they need to correct and when they don't are developing functional correction strategies. The strategies must be theirs. When *they* realize something has gone wrong, *they* will take the opportunity to locate the problem and fix it. There's no good reason to call their attention to miscues that don't disrupt the process of making sense.

Short-circuiting the reading process

As these strategies show, and as I've stressed again and again in this book, the process of reading is focussed on making sense of print. And if the process gets short-circuited, sense is lost. That can happen to any of us if we try to read a text to which we bring insufficient background knowledge. We can often produce an oral rendition of the text that sounds as if we understand it, even though we don't. Then oral reading becomes a performance more than an attempt to get to meaning. Skillful readers use as much of the reading process as they can when they face an incomprehensible text: signal, syntax, wording. They try to assign appropriate intonation. But they have only fragments of meaning — and they're not sure what to make of those.

For less sophisticated readers, the reading process is sometimes short-circuited by instruction. Instruction that strongly focusses on letter/sound matching or word identification can teach developing readers that the goal of reading is to decode print as sound, or to recognize a succession of words. Isolated phonics produces what some British folks have called "barking at print." Short-circuiting at the word level produces the monotone reading of a text as nothing more than a list of words. Only when the focus of the reader, at whatever level of proficiency, is on meaning is the whole process at work and short-circuiting minimized.

Summary

By calling reading a psycholinguistic guessing game, I wanted to emphasize the active role of the reader in making sense of written language as a new key element in our understanding of the reading process. I wanted people to take distance from the view that reading is the accurate, sequential recognition of letters and words. I wanted them to understand that, in order to make sense (construct meaning), readers:

➤ make continuous use of minimal information selected from a complex but incomplete and ambiguous text;

➤ draw on their knowledge of language and the world;

➤ use strategies of predicting and inferring where the text is going.

In short, I wanted them to understand that readers engage in informed guessing as they read.

I've devoted many years of research and thinking to explicating and understanding the process of reading more precisely. In the previous chapter I examined the nature of a written text: its three basic levels, how the cues are organized by the writer in composing the text, and what the reader must bring to the text to make sense of it. In this chapter I described the process as cyclical, starting with vision and ending with meaning. I also described the psycholinguistic strategies that readers use in the guessing game.

I've provided all of this detail to assure you that reading has been studied in depth for many decades, and we now know with considerable understanding what readers do to make sense of a text. Although there is surely more to learn, the reading guessing game is no mystery. We've learned a lot since 1967.

Still, we'll never know it all. Reading is a dynamic unity, a process people use for important personal and social reasons. Walt Whitman once wrote a poem titled "When I Heard the Learn'd Astronomer," included in a collection of his poems selected by Lawrence Powell (1964). It goes like this:

> When I heard the learn'd astronomer,
> When the proofs, the figures, were ranged in columns before
>   me,
> When I was shown the charts and diagrams, to add, divide, and
>   measure them,
> When I sitting heard the astronomer where he lectures with
>   much applause in the lecture-room,
> How soon unaccountable I became tired and sick,
> Till rising and gliding out I wander'd off by myself,
> In the mystical moist night-air, and from time to time,
> Look'd up in perfect silence at the stars.

To me, Whitman seems to be saying that knowing scientifically about stars doesn't fit with his poet's wonder at them. Reading is wonderful. The unique human ability to use language — oral, written, sign — to communicate poetic feelings, marvelous ideas and scientific understandings is wonderful. Understanding how reading works scientifically doesn't make this human achievement less wonderful.

Nor does it mean that we who are educators should use this scientific knowledge to turn reading into something less than wonderful for young learners. Understanding how reading works should help us to comprehend how reading is learned and to create and support school programs that help children become "wonderful" readers.

8

*Teaching
can support and
extend learning, but it can
never make it
happen.*

Learning and teaching reading and writing

I plan to focus on teaching and learning in another book, but it seems to me that I owe you, here, some sense of what I believe. What we've learned about written language processes has major implications for understanding how written language is learned, and for building a pedagogy: a principled stance for the teaching of reading and writing. Fortunately, a rich professional literature already exists on that topic. Many teachers have already put into practice what we know about literacy processes, and some have had their teaching stories published. You'll find a representative bibliography at the end of this book.

Let me make two things perfectly clear at the start:

➤ There is simply no *direct* connection between knowing about language competence and understanding how that knowledge is developed, or how to teach it.

➤ The relationship between theory and practice is a two-way street.

First, it seems obvious that teaching reading and writing requires knowing what competent reading and writing is. A sound approach to teaching must be consistent with and build on a scientific knowledge of literacy and how it is learned, but it must also build on knowledge of language development, sound learning theories, and an understanding of teaching and curriculum.

Second, educators don't just apply knowledge, they produce it. Classroom teachers have taught me a lot about learning and teaching literacy; they've also taught me a lot about the reading process in the real world of classrooms — knowledge that researchers and theoreticians need to add to what they learn under research conditions. Whole language teachers have taken control of the body of knowledge about how reading and writing work and have built their own pedagogy on that knowledge — their teaching theory and practice. What we know is important for teaching, but who knows it and what they do with the knowledge is even more important.

Later in this chapter that point is demonstrated in four classroom vignettes that show teachers playing a much wider range of roles than "direct instruction" entails. But first I'll describe how literacy begins and develops in literate societies.

Growing into literacy in a literate environment

A baby is born. Anxious parents are reassured by doctors and nurses that the baby is "healthy and normal." In comparison with most animal babies, human babies are born quite helpless and immature; it takes them a long time to be able to do the things adults do. But their proud parents are patient and confident that in due course they will smile, turn themselves over, sit up, crawl, stand, walk, and so on. Given a nurturing home and normal human associations, the baby will grow, develop, change and learn. (Of course I know that not all babies are born normal in every respect, but we need to understand normal development before we can understand the abnormal development of a few children.)

In due course, human infants also begin to understand the spoken language around them, and to speak it themselves. Because it happens as naturally as standing and walking, it seems like just another result of their physical maturation. But that's only partly true; other animals have the same control over the sound-producing organs, but only human beings develop language. Human language is qualitatively different from the rudimentary, limited communication of other animal species.

What makes language both necessary and possible is that our brains have the ability to think symbolically: we let things represent other things. Because we can create complex abstract systems for representing the most subtle experiences, concepts and ideas, we are able to reflect on our experiences and communicate our needs, experiences and ideas to others. All human societies, at all times in recorded history and before, have created and used oral language.

That doesn't mean that no learning is involved, of course. But learning language is different in important ways from learning to walk, and from the learning of other animals. Human language learning is *both personal and social*. It is the medium for thought and learning, but also, since we are born dependent, our survival and development depend on our ability to join a social dialog as we join a social community. So, language is essential not only for our physical and social survival, but also for our sharing in the collective knowledge of our families, communities and societies.

Written language is learned a little later in the life of individuals and societies, but it is no less natural than oral language in the personal and social development of human beings. And the process by which written language develops is the same as that for oral language development. Both develop out of the need of humans to think symbolically and to communicate in a growing range of contexts and functions, as individuals and as societies. Written language is an extension of human language development that occurs when it's needed: when face-to-face and here-and-now language is no longer sufficient.

We've learned a lot over the last few decades about how children develop as readers and writers. What it took was a liberation from the mistaken view that written language learning is fundamentally different from oral language learning, a view that led to the equally mistaken notion that literacy learning begins when children enter school. As a result, most of us, including parents, simply didn't see the literacy learning going on all around us. As Yetta Goodman says, generations of parents have washed off their walls the evidence of their children's writing development. The truth is that children come to school already rich in literacy experiences, and having already learned to make sense of print.

As we take a look at schools in this chapter, you need to keep in mind that, while I separate *learning* reading and writing from *teaching* reading and writing, I can't do so absolutely. Children continue to learn to read and write while they're receiving instruction, and it's hard to separate the results of learning from the results of instruction. Also, some of what parents and others do outside of school can be seen as instructional, even when instruction isn't explicitly intended — for example, when a child shows a parent a box of cereal, points to the print and says, "What does this say?" In his study of his son's language development, Halliday (1971) identified a phenomena he called "tracking": the child takes the lead in language development and the parent follows and supports that development. Children and parents do it all the time.

In any case, instructional programs in school must build on the beginnings children have already made. Instead of regarding the reading-writing curriculum as a set of new skills children have to learn, teachers have to recognize and build on the development already taking place. Classrooms ought to be richly literate environments, providing lots of support for extending and strengthening the literacy development that began before the children ever entered school.

Language acquisition and development

I need to digress briefly to put my view of learning, particularly literacy learning, in context. Two views of human language learning are commonly contrasted: "nature" vs. "nurture." These, and my own view, can be described as follows:

➤ In the "nature" view, language is considered innate. It's not learned at all, but acquired by bringing the innate, universal language into harmony with the particular language community the child is born into. For many who hold this view, only oral language is innate, written language an abstract representation of it. Written language is acquired through instruction.

➤ The "nurture" view is mainly a behaviorist approach. In it, language, like everything else, is learned through some kind of operant conditioning. Environmental stimuli require responses, and somehow in the process language is shaped.

➤ "Invention and convention" is what I label my own view, which draws on the work of the Russian psychologist Lev Vygotsky, the Swiss psychologist Jean Piaget and the Anglo-Australian linguist Michael Halliday.

I see human learning, including language learning, as *a process of invention*. Human beings invent (socially construct) language to communicate with each other and to learn and think with. Language is therefore a social invention. But since society is made up of people, it is also a personal invention. In fact, we each individually invent language and keep inventing it throughout our lives.

But we invent our own language within a family and community which already have a language loaded with the *conventional* ways of doing the things we are inventing. Piaget calls this kind of tension "disequilibrium." Our personal inventions and the social conventions of the language of the people around us pull and push us in opposite directions. As Vygotsky puts it (1978), our personal language moves toward the social language until, eventually, we appear to have "internalized" the latter. At that point, the social language becomes the basis for our inner speech, the language we use for learning and for reflecting on experience.

As we move toward conventional language, we also come to share the values and life views of our family and society. Halliday called the book in which he presented his research on language development *Learning How to Mean*. We learn how our culture organizes and expresses meaning through language. Language is learned in the process of its use, through participation in speech acts and literacy events. Lots of participation in talk is what makes it possible for children to learn oral language. And lots of writing and reading make it possible for children to build written language.

Building on what children know

Surrounded by print in a literate society, children become aware that written language is a way of making sense. They begin very early to respond to print as meaningful, recognizing logos and signs as a way of identifying places and products: a stop sign or the Golden Arches, for example. Gradually they learn, in succession: that print makes sense, what sense print makes, how print makes sense — that is, they come to control the system of written language. Children play at the activities of the adults around them, and much of their early literacy is developed in playing at reading and writing. Yetta Goodman and others, in many places and languages, have documented how children first invent written language and then move toward the conventions.

In literate societies, some children move easily into literacy. They write notes and cards (which adults often can't read), compose shopping lists, create signs (KEP AWT) to put on their bedroom door, read "McDonald's," "CREST" and "Sesame Street." By the time they enter school, they read and write more or less conventionally. Most other children, through their transactions with print in the environment, have at least begun their journey into literacy, and many are well into it.

Learning to transact with text

As we've discovered, reading and writing is making sense by transacting with text, using the three systems of language simultaneously. So what is it that children must learn to do? Essentially, they must develop strategies and learn to use textual cues to make sense of text — that is, construct meaning. They can do that only by transacting with real texts in which the three systems of language relate authentically to each other. They can't learn to control written language by focussing separately on each system. They can't learn phonics, vocabulary and grammar in isolation because, in the real world, those systems don't occur in isolation from language or from each other. Just as children learn to talk and listen in authentic oral language settings, they learn to read and write in authentic literacy settings.

Only in the context of real language do the graphophonic, lexico-grammatic and semantic language systems occur in the proper relationships so that young learners can develop and use strategies for making sense. They need to learn to sample the print selectively, predict and infer, and self-correct as needed, all within a focus on making sense of print. And as they develop these strategies, they need to become confident in playing the psycholinguistic guessing game — getting to meaning with minimal effort and input. On the other hand, they need to be cautious enough that they can monitor their good guesses and make sure they fit the developing text. Finding a balance between confidence and tentativeness is essential to reading development.

Building a sense of text

As successful users of oral language, children know how various kinds of texts work — that conversations involve turn-taking, for instance. Written language extends and builds on this sense of text — certain kinds of stories begin with *Once upon a time* and end with *lived happily ever after*. Control of the forms of the different kinds of texts (genres) depends on having considerable experience with using them functionally. There are no shortcuts in this process; the form develops in the context of functional use over time.

The convention of word spacing, for example, comes early in children's writing, but word spacing depends on a sense of "wordness," and that's not simple. Even mature writers produce anomalies: *alot (a lot), anotherwards (in other words), all ready (already), spit and image (spitting image)*. When to hyphenate is not always clear, even to the most literate — when *whole language* and when *whole-language*? It's useful to think of language as composed of discrete words, but it takes a lot of experience to know when one word stops and another begins. It took centuries before word spacing in alphabetic writing was introduced, as we can see in medieval manuscripts.

Readers and writers must also have a sense of sentence before they can punctuate conventionally, a sense that research shows is still developing through fourth grade (Goodman and Wilde, 1994). Children use sentences in their speech and in their writing, but their sense of sentence is not developed enough for them to punctuate conventionally on a consistent basis. Their punctuation system doesn't match adult conventions until they acquire a conventional view of sentences, and that takes lots of reading and writing.

Inventing the spelling system

I've defined phonics as the set of relationships between someone's oral language sound system (phonology) and the spelling and punctuation of the language (orthography). When children (or adults) learn to read and write, they invent a personal phonics system that relates their own speech system to English spelling.

English, like almost all alphabetically written languages, has spellings that are standardized across dialects. To connect their personal sound system to these standardized spellings, beginning writers invent rules as they write. These rules produce possible spellings, based on the way the writers hear the words in their own speech communities. But they don't produce standard spellings because, to be standard across all dialects, spellings can't relate specifically to the sound systems of any one dialect. The good news is that these beginning writers are soon able to write anything they want to say using the personal spelling rules they've developed — and willing parents, teachers and others can make sense of the kids' writing even if it's filled with invented spellings.

The bad news is that moving from readable invented spellings to standard conventional spellings takes a long time. The English spelling system has so many different roots that even literate, well-educated adults rarely come close to being "perfect spellers." That's why word processors have spell-checkers. It's why winning a spelling bee is a great achievement. And it's why adults habitually avoid using certain words they aren't sure they can spell. It's likely that the combined forces of my own care, a good spell-checker and the attentive work of editors and proofreaders won't prevent some of my unconventional spellings from finding their way into the printed version of this book. Blame the complexity of English spellings. But also give credit to the wonder of language, which leads even proofreaders into reading for meaning instead of attending to the spelling details of every word.

Reading and writing are the major roadways to conventional spelling. Ideally, children should begin writing as early as they begin reading. Writers read like writers — as they read, they notice the conventional spellings of words they've used or want to use in their writing, and then they use those words they've noticed in their reading to move toward conventional spelling in their writing.

How vocabulary is built

One simplistic view of language is that it's just a set of words — and, if so, learning a language is just building a large vocabulary, and learning to read and write is just learning the written language vocabulary. But I disagree and say again: *words are definable only in specific language contexts*. Dictionary makers start with many specific uses of a word by real people, then cross-reference them to build definitions. Young children learn word meanings the same way: they hear the same words in many different utterances and form a sense of meaning from what is common across these utterances. They begin to use specific words in contexts like the ones they've heard them in, and then move toward using them in new utterances when they seem appropriate.

Children often use a right word in the wrong context, like "wait a few whiles" from one three-year-old. Second-language learners do the same as they take risks in expressing themselves in their new language. In both cases, the vocabulary develops as less familiar words are used in invented expressions. We build our vocabulary, in both oral and written language, through much experience with using it. There are no shortcuts that can give us the words we need before we need them. We encounter new words, or new uses of words, in our reading and listening, and then we begin to use the words ourselves. Some researchers have concluded that a large vocabulary is a *prerequisite* of proficient reading, but they're wrong: vocabulary is the *result* of reading.

One lesson this teaches us about literacy development is that, in the transaction between reader and text, the text acts as a mediator. The author has used certain words, phrases, syntax, style, and the reader's construction of text and meaning is mediated by the elements of the published text. When we ask readers to retell a story they've just read, they reconstruct the text using words, phrases and stylistic devices the text used — which isn't surprising, since the retelling usually follows right after the reading. But it's also true that readers often use elements from recent reading in their own speaking and writing. In other words, readers are changed by their transactions with texts: their reading/writing development is affected by the texts they are reading. That's one more reason why developing readers need to have a diet of authentic texts in which words occur in their normal rich diversity.

Learning by doing

Learning language is so universal that people must find it easy to do.

"Learning by doing" is John Dewey's term for the way we acquire knowledge in the process of doing necessary things. Since language is a complex, abstract system for representing meaning, learning it should be difficult. But language is learned so universally that it can't be difficult.

The key is that the learning is done in the context of activities in which language is necessary. It's easy to see how kids are immersed in activities that require oral language; it took us longer to realize that in literate societies they are also immersed in written language activities, and that they learn as easily and universally from those activities. We can conclude that language is learned most easily when the focus isn't on the language but on what we're doing with it.

Moreover, just as we learn to talk by listening, we learn to write by reading. In each case, we become aware of the system of language by trying to make sense of it over many experiences. We invent our own systems for speaking and writing, drawing on the resources from our listening and reading. Gradually our inventions for expressing our meanings move toward the conventions of the social language, oral or written. Oral language supports written language because the two share grammar and meanings. We build written language with all of the oral language resources. Receptive processes support productive ones, and vice versa.

Usually, receptive language moves ahead of productive — we understand more oral language than we can produce as we learn first and second languages. For most, reading develops faster than writing, but there are some exceptions. Children encouraged to use invented spellings reach a point where they can write anything they choose to because they have a system for inventing spellings for words they don't know how to spell conventionally. However, they may be less confident about their ability to read unfamiliar texts.

For those already literate in one language and learning a second, reading may be the first process to develop — even before listening. They use their first-language literacy to make sense of the new language, puzzling through a written text until it makes sense. In the process, they learn the grammar and word meanings of the second language and begin to invent the oral language by using what they're learning in the reading.

Learning in and out of school

Language learning is language learning. There isn't a school kind and a not-school kind. Learning activities in school should be just as meaningful, just as functional, just as authentic as those out of school. The only difference is that in school there's a teacher and a large group of kids — in other words, a community of learners with opportunities to use language together in solving real problems and posing and answering real questions.

In such an environment, all the language systems are present, the vocabulary is appropriate and varied, and the language is learned in the context of using it. Language activities are authentic because they exist for real purposes and not just for instruction, and that's the key to learning written language with ease: the literacy events focus on authentic texts and authentic tasks.

Lifelong learning

Each of us continues to develop language, both oral and written, over our whole lives, as we encounter new experiences and new needs. Every new interest creates a need for new language. We continue to learn new language every time we experience a new hobby: knitting, bowling, computers; a new class or curriculum: biology, algebra, medicine; a new place: climate, people, traditions.

What's wonderful about our human ability to invent language, individually and socially, is that it never ends. Some people have argued that there's a short, critical period early in human life when language is learned with remarkable ease, after which the learning is much harder. To reach this conclusion, they compare the remarkable speed of early language development with the relative slowness adults show in learning second languages. But what accounts for that difference is simply that most adults shy away from the risks involved in trying out their inventions as they move toward language conventions.

Language grows and changes continuously throughout human life to serve new needs in new contexts. We stretch our vocabularies, refine and modify our grammar, even change our speech sounds as we encounter new needs, situations and interactions with others. Early language development is truly remarkable, but how limited human thought, learning and communication would be if we were limited to what we could learn during the first few years of life!

Literacy and illiteracy

Before we shift our focus from learning to teaching, let's consider the realities of who learns and who doesn't learn to be literate. With very rare exceptions, anyone who is capable of learning oral language is also capable of learning written language. In fact, because written language shares the syntax and meaning structures of oral language, it ought to be easier to learn than learning oral language is for infants, just as it should be easier to learn to read and write a second language if you're already literate in your first language.

Yet many children appear slow in controlling reading and writing, do poorly in school programs and score poorly on tests. Even some literate adults score poorly on literacy and minimal competency tests. Periodically, claims are made that literacy is declining, that our students aren't as literate as those in the past and in other countries. (Interestingly, the same claims are made in most literate countries, especially those doing lots of testing.) And who are the low achievers, on the whole? The record is clear: the poor, the immigrants, the racial and ethnic minorities. Also, far more boys than girls wind up in remedial reading programs.

New Zealand researcher Warwick Elley recently directed a 21-nation study of reading. His report, *How in the World Do Students Read?*, is available from the US Department of Education. In general, the United States and Canada compare well with other developed nations, although they show complex literacy patterns because of their mixed populations. Most Scandinavian countries come out high for three reasons: relatively homogeneous populations, superb humanistic schools and, ironically, television — because American programs are broadcast in English with subtitles in the Scandinavian language, children do a lot of reading as they watch television. The lowest results came from third-world countries that spend far less on education.

New Zealand was at the top of earlier international studies of literacy, but in this study it has fallen a few places. Elley's careful analysis of his data shows some interesting insights — recent immigrants from other parts of Polynesia tend to test lower than native Maoris, for example. A calm, dispassionate view of such test data can suggest further investigation and some school and community responses.

In today's world, although the percentage of illiteracy is declining, the actual number of illiterates is increasing, mostly because of high birth rates in the poorest countries and the poorest areas within countries. Overall literacy rates are increasing in proportion to the amounts of national income spent on education and changes in economic conditions. Perhaps the most significant fact is that people everywhere are literate more or less in proportion to their need and opportunity to be literate, since functional need is the driving force behind language development. Literacy campaigns work where the conditions of life make literacy necessary and possible; they have little permanent effect where there's little opportunity for using literacy.

For years I've been relating a vignette from Debra Goodman's teaching. She was discussing with a group of inner-city fourth-graders how they learned to ride bikes, comparing that with how they had learned to read and write. After some discussion they agreed on these key aspects:

➤ You have to really want to ride a bike. Teachers call that personal motivation.

➤ You have to practice a lot. That means getting on and riding, not practicing component skills such as steering and pedaling.

➤ You have to be willing to fall off a lot. That's called risk-taking: learning involves bumps and bruises.

A man in one audience in Caracas, Venezuela, suggested an important additional condition: you have to have access to a bicycle. Just as you can't learn to ride a bike if you can't get the use of one, you can't learn to read and write without access to authentic reading and writing. This helps us to understand who in the world and in our societies is illiterate — and to consider the value of instructional programs in which kids are denied access to real reading and writing.

Blaming the victim

In the common cyclical revival of "the reading crisis in North America," the learners are often blamed for the failures of the educational system. We assume something is "wrong" with them and devise test after test to find out what. Given enough tests, of course, we can find something wrong with anyone. Recently the press reported an interesting controversy surrounding an exclusive private school for gifted students. A well-meaning philanthropist had provided enormous funding to provide testing, counseling and remediation for those students identified by a massive staff of psychologists and other specialists as having reading and learning disabilities. The majority of the students were identified as handicapped and subjected to corrective treatment! This idiocy was questioned only when some of the teachers had enough and refused to cooperate.

My own view is that every failure of a child is a failure of the school. In the case of learning to read and write, appropriate, well-planned instruction by professional teachers can assure virtually universal success. What it takes is the learners' ownership of their own literacy.

On one early morning flight I heard a comedian recount a tale that could have been from my own childhood. "Little Orphan Annie" was a radio program for kids, sponsored by Ovaltine. After each episode the announcer would promise that if you sent in a quarter and the inner seal of an Ovaltine jar, you would receive a decoder ring to decode the secret message given at the end of each program. The comedian coaxed his mother to buy the Ovaltine, saved his pennies, traded them for a quarter and sent them in. After weeks, the ring arrived. He rushed home from school, waited impatiently for the secret message after the program and eagerly used the ring to decode the secret message. The message? "Drink Ovaltine."

I've often thought of that as a metaphor for many ineffective school reading programs: when you're finally able to make some sense of something in the basal reader, it's a sponsor's message, not your own. If reading and writing are to be learned easily and well, the learners must have ownership over the process and its results. What they understand from their reading must be interesting and useful to them. It must bring pleasure, information, answers to their own questions. Learning is difficult if it has no present utility for the learners.

Developing literacy: a case in point

We know quite a lot about the development children go through to reach the point where they are comprehensible if not conventional writers. Through a large body of research we know that what Yetta Goodman calls "the roots of literacy" are usually characterized by changes in children's attempts at writing. There are various reasons for these changes. The purpose of this section is to illustrate the process with an account based on Prisca Martens' doctoral study of her daughter, Sarah, from her first beginnings of reading and writing until she entered kindergarten, from ages two to five. (A book based on this study is in press.) Sarah's development is representative of what happens in children in general.

In her infancy Sarah watched her mother and father read notes, newspapers, recipes and mail and write grocery lists, checks, letters and papers for graduate school. She watched Matthew, three years older, read books, logos, signs and magazines and write signs, stories and greeting cards. Immersed in a literate family in a literate community, Sarah became aware of the social and then the communicative functions of written language.

She had easy access to materials and would write intently from the time she could hold a pencil or marker. She saw herself as a writer even in her earliest efforts. Her first inventions were lines and circles, elements she perceived as part of the written language around her. Initially she referred to her circles as "ohs." Soon her circles moved from just being marks to being placeholders for meaning.

The first example on the opposite page shows Sarah's use of placeholders and how she read them. She may be reflecting a principle Ferreiro and Teberosky report from their Piagetian research (1982), that children expect big things to look

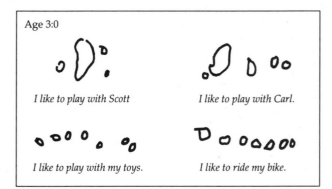

Age 3:0

I like to play with Scott   *I like to play with Carl.*

I like to play with my toys.   *I like to ride my bike.*

bigger in print. Carl and Scott were big boys and her use of large Os to represent them may express her sense of their size.

One morning, while making a birthday card, she invented a new system: she used one letter to represent each syllable or word as she spoke it. Ferreiro and Teberosky call this the "syllabic hypothesis" (some syllabic writing systems are in use in Asia and other places). For the next month, Sarah used the syllabic hypothesis whenever she wrote.

Age 3:4

Hap-py Birth-day

I love Matthew

I love Grandpa   Age 3:4

Age 3:5

a I D h I L t t t
I like some guh-uh-uh-uh-uh grass

I T D h   a   h
I like Moh-uh-uh-my

But then she modified this principle: she elongated key syllables by using more letters and giving each letter part of the sound. The following month she moved to an alphabetic principle, using one letter for each sound she heard. This relatively rapid development was entirely her own progression.

Up to this point her writing samples seem to lack creativity. Although she was already identifying many letters, she used few in her writing, in relatively fixed arrangements. And all of her writing, except birthday cards, were sentences beginning "I like . . ." or "I love . . ." Her use of writing was less communicative than social — a way of expressing personal relationship. Other than some awareness of word and sentence length, her focus was less on the form of the language around her than on its social function.

When she entered preschool, Sarah developed an intense interest in her name. She spelled it orally and delighted in finding "her" letters in print in her environment. Just one week after this interest began, she picked up a marker and wrote her name, using a capital <S> but minuscule letters for the rest, as her mother had demonstrated.

She quickly began experimenting with directionality in her name. The English writing system is written left to right on the page, as are most letters. In beginning writers, letter directionality depends on where the young writer begins each letter (top left, top right, lower left, lower right). In "Sarah" the <a>s face right but are written right to left (circle then stick). The <S> is tricky because it starts at the upper right and is written right to left.

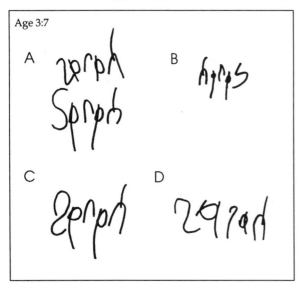

Age 3:7

A B C D

For three weeks (see A in the sample), Sarah's <S> was as likely to go right to left as left to right. She formed her <a>s by making a circle and then a stick, but she put the stick before the circle. The <r> was conventional, but she put the stick for the <h> in the middle of the hump.

Then she went into a four-day period (B) when she would write her whole name in either direction, producing mirror versions when she started at the right and wrote to the left. She had the sequence under control, but not the direction. Her <S> remained conventional, however.

After that (C), she always wrote from left to right; her <S> consistently went from left to right as well. Finally (D), she arrived at the version she used as her signature for the next year, reversing not only the <S> but also the <r> and the <h>. It was her name, her personal sign, her written identity.

The next change in Sarah's name writing came months later: a sudden shift to using all capitals. She sometimes mixed upper- and lower-case letters in her other writing, but never in her name.

Age 3:7-3:11

Once she had a signature for herself, she moved to fixed forms for Matthew, Mommy and Daddy. These were the only words she wrote that didn't employ invented spelling.

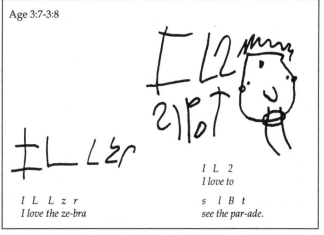

Age 3:7-3:8

I L L z r
I love the ze-bra

I L 2
I love to

s l B t
see the par-ade.

During this same time period, the messages on her notes, pictures and cards began appearing with the first or a prominent sound in each syllable or word.

Sarah

DeY AsBos
Dear Ambrose

VA u vo v TAKc
Thank you for the tickets.

I LIK V
I like the

KYL
gorilla.

I LIK V SIN
I like the Suns.

Age 4:5

Gradually she moved to using patterns of letters to represent patterns of sounds she heard. This example of her early alphabetic writing is in the form of a thank-you note. It reflects her perceptions of the sound patterns of her oral language and her inventions for spelling those patterns in her writing. At this stage she represented the /r/ sound as /w/in her speech, and in writing she represented it with <y>. She said "fank" for "thank" and "fuh" for "the" and spelled both initial sounds with <v>. (The /v/ and /f/ sounds are closely related.) She was using the letter <c> for /s/ sounds and <k> for the /g/ in "gorilla" (again closely related sounds). She consistently represented the schwa she heard in "Suns" with an <I>. What may look at first like bizarre spelling is actually relatively systematic and consistent, reflecting her keen hearing and her active invention of phonic relationships.

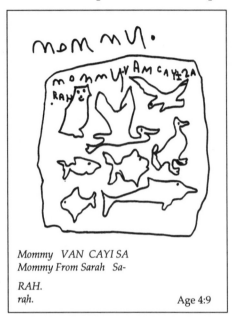

Mommy VAN CAYI SA
Mommy From Sarah Sa-

RAH.
rah.   Age 4:9

Fifteen months after she began writing her name, she handed her mother a stencilled picture, which she read: "Mommy, from S-a-w-uh, Sarah," emphasizing each sound she had represented in writing before saying her name. She had invented a spelling for her name — <C> for /s/, <A> for /æ/, <Y> for /w/ and <I> for /ə/ — but she still added her signature, SARAH. She used different letters for the different sounds that <a> represents in the conventional spelling of her name. She only heard four sounds so she needed only four letters.

Five weeks after her first invention, Sarah modified it to ZAYRI. She inserted an <R>, which she saw in her conventionally printed name, but still retained the <Y> for /w/ — perhaps she simply wanted there to be five letters. And she used <Z> rather than <C> for /s/. She was using both sound and sight in inventing her spellings.

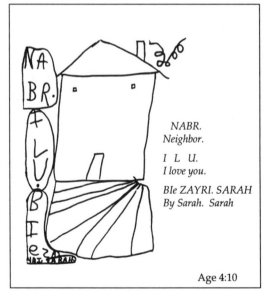

NABR.
Neighbor.

I L U.
I love you.

Ble ZAYRI. SARAH
By Sarah. Sarah

                                    Age 4:10

At the same time, she was creating invented spellings for the other family names that, until then, she had been spelling conventionally. She was using her own invented rules rather than holistic representations, which shows

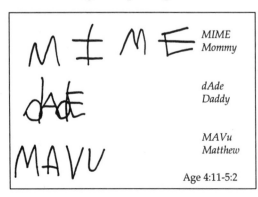

MIME
Mommy

dAde
Daddy

MAVu
Matthew

Age 4:11-5:2

her confidence in them. She'd learned that there are rules for language and was using her personal spelling rules for everything she wrote. She hadn't yet come to grips with the ways conventional English spelling compromises rules in order to be standard across all personal and social forms of the language.

Sarah's continued invention of English spelling liberated her to write. She had a sense that she could say in writing anything she wanted to or needed to say. Before long, her invented spellings reached the point where anyone could comprehend them. She added punctuation (invented but moving toward conventional) and began to experiment with different genres as she needed them: maps, thank-you notes, playing school, lists and charts. Before starting kindergarten, Sarah had become a writer. Neither she nor her parents ever doubted that she would be.

Sarah is a unique child, but her remarkable development as a writer (and reader) is not unique. Because her mother kept all the evidence of her writing development, we know her story. But, with much variation in pace, timeframe and sequence, the process is the same for all children as they become literate.

Our story ends with Sarah starting kindergarten at age five. Much to her parents' distress, her first school experience did not extend this strong beginning. Her teacher was locked into readiness and part-to-whole instruction, and Sarah's reading and writing was confined to exercises on letters and words and phonics drills. She was often in trouble because she turned over the worksheets, drew a picture and wrote her own story. The teacher seemed unaware that Sarah and some of her classmates were already readers and writers. She saw her job as getting children ready for the skill-and-drill instruction that would make them readers and writers.

At the end of one semester the family moved and Sarah entered a whole-language kindergarten. Her new teacher, Wendy Hood, writes this description of Sarah's first day in her classroom:

> Sarah joined my kindergarten in January, the first day back from winter break. She arrived, backpack full, brand new stuffed Dalmatian puppy under her arm. She stopped at the easel just outside the door, watching momentarily as other students signed in on the easel. Then she signed her own and her puppy's name.

> I greeted all the children with hugs and new blank journals. As the students settled in, Sarah asked timidly if she could use her own writing tools. In her old school, she said, she could only use the pencils and crayons provided. Permission granted, Sarah chose a seat and began to empty colored pencils, markers, glitter crayons and more from her well-organized pack. "Want to share?" she said to the others.

Sarah drew a detailed picture in her new journal and wrote about it. I could read her writing. In my anecdotal record book I noted: *Sarah M. January 7. First day in our classroom. Writes first and last names. Generates invented spelling that is readable, consistently left to right, some appropriate word spacing. Seems to be very phonetic, based on her own speech patterns.*

Journal time over, we had a large-group time. We welcomed Sarah as a new member of our community. We sang our favorite friendship songs for her. She listened well and shared willingly as the kids were invited to talk about their holidays.

As I held up the book I was going to read to the class, Sarah quietly whispered, "Happy Birthday." "Yes, Sarah," I replied, "this says, 'Happy Birthday.' Do you know whose birthday is coming up?"

Sarah and her classmates looked at the book, *Happy Birthday, Martin Luther King*, and tried to guess. "My brother's name starts like that. Matthew starts like that name," Sarah said, worming closer to the front of the room. Classmate Michelle tentatively said, "Martin Luther King?" "Yes, that's right," I responded. "Let's read the title of the book together." Sarah and Michelle had two of the strongest voices as the class read the title with me.

In my anecdotal record book I noted: *Sarah read "Happy Birthday" from the title of the book. It's obvious she's reading other things as well. Find time for a miscue analysis in the next few days.*

How teaching supports learning

Wendy Hood understands that her job is to help learners take off from where they are when they come to her. She takes it for granted that her kindergarten children are already reaching toward literacy. She takes pains to involve them in literacy events, watches them carefully and notes where they are in their development. Then she stimulates further development without taking ownership away from her charges.

Like many other teachers, she believes that if you want to teach kids, you need to be a *kid*-watcher. If humans learned like rats and pigeons, experiments with rats and pigeons would be valid. In fact, children *can* learn like rats and pigeons, but the reverse isn't true: rats and pigeons can't learn like children. Children learn the same ways in and out of school — teachers don't have to restrict their teaching to telling the children directly what they must know. They don't have to cut up teaching and learning into measurable bite-size pieces and arrange sequenced bits into instructional programs, the way basal readers do.

Unlike rats and pigeons, humans possess the ability to learn language and to use language in learning. We use language not only to share our insights and experiences, but also to reflect on our experiences and learn from them. If teachers have a deep appreciation of the universal ability of children to learn and use functional written language, and a basic understanding of how written language works, then a very different kind of classroom emerges, one in which the teacher *supports* learners as they move into reading and writing by building on their language strengths.

Wendy Hood calls herself a whole language teacher. Whole language has emerged as a complete pedagogy, rich, diverse and complex. The following vignettes illustrate what teachers and learners in a whole language classroom do as they build literacy. Each is a true story.

When are we going to have reading?

This vignette was written by Debra Goodman, a former middle-grades teacher at the Dewey Center for Urban Education, a magnet school in inner-city Detroit, MI. Key activities are represented in italic.

In the math center, several students are *staring at post-it labels* clustered under the headings "Basketball" and "Freeze Tag." Jay is *reading to the group* from the book *Sideways Arithmetic at Wayside School.*

"Oh," says Marcella, "I thought you said 'cheese tag.'. . . I LOVE freeze tag."
    Demetrius says, "OK. Well, if Marcella plays freeze tag, then Janice will too. She does anything Marcella does."
    "And there goes Freda," says Renata. "She said she'd only play basketball if there were ten people."

Steven, a new student, is instructed to move the names from "Basketball" to "Freeze Tag." Jay then goes *back to the book to read more* as the group collaborates to *solve the puzzle the book has posed.*

Elsewhere, the Art Committee is meeting. Meagan and Ben are *making a sign* titled "Rules for the Art Committee." The rules are:
    1. There are no rules.
    2. Pay attention to rule #1.

John looks up from his poster — a pencil puncturing a basketball, meant to demonstrate that the Art Committee is more important than the Sports Committee. "I think we should have real rules," he says. Tamika looks up from *filling out the weekly committee report* and the discussion begins.

In the Sports Center, Bethany is *organizing books and materials.* As she puts the books away, she looks at the cover and then *flips through each book,* sometimes stopping to *read or examine an illustration*. At times she comments to Heather who is *reading a book* called *Teammates* and thinking about Jackie Robinson. "You won't believe this," says Heather. "He couldn't even stay in the same hotel with the other players." Bethany stops to *read the book* with Heather.

I am also in the Sports Center, working with Derek who's been having some trouble with his research. Together we've been *reading* about the origins of soccer. I put the book aside and ask Derek what important or interesting facts he'd like to remember. "Put down how warriors would kick heads around the field after the battle," Derek says. I *act as scribe* as we list the salient facts.

Meanwhile, three boys are *sitting in the reading corner* surrounded by Matt Christopher's books. They are *talking about the books they've read* and *deciding which books they want to read next*. They *consult the bulletin board* where a chart entitled "Matt Christopher Fan Club" has a place for the club members to *check off the books they've read*. They get a little noisy, and Monique looks up from her Babysitter's Club book. "Be quiet," she says. "I'm *trying to read*." Anthony never looks up from *the thick fantasy book he's engrossed in*.

In the Science Center, six students are *reading instructions* for a fitness experiment. Julia, a member of the Science Committee, answers their questions if they become confused. After *reading the instructions*, they sit quietly for 30 seconds and then Julia helps them find their pulse rate and *record it on a worksheet*. The group moves out into the hallway to examine walking and running pulse rates.

John and Donavan have been circulating around the room with their *survey question*: "What is your favorite sport?" They return to the open work area to discuss their data. After talking over the responses, they begin to *organize the information on a survey tally sheet*. Carol sits near them *writing a letter* to the editor of *Sports Illustrated* protesting their lack of serious attention to women as athletes rather than sex objects, as in the swimsuit edition. A stack of magazines are piled next to her and she *refers to them* from time to time. Other students are *looking through the same magazines* for articles related to their research questions.

At the writing conference table, Lisa and Eli listen as Reuben *reads a poem* about swimming. Eli says it reminds him of some of Arnold Adoff's poems and he runs over to the Sports Center to *find the book*.

At the listening post near the Sports Center, Sam and Daniel are listening to a taped interview of a local athlete who visited the classroom. They *look over the notes in their thinking journals*. They *read the notes that have been written on post-its* and posted around the listening post carrel, and they *write out some comments* of their own.

Sharon throws up her hands in frustration from the desk where she's been *looking through a stack of books for information*. She walks over to the secretar; desk to *sign up for a research conference*. Kenneth, the classroom secretary for the day, *finds the right folder* for Sharon and *crosses her name off the pencil list* as she returns her pencil and goes to put her books away. When Barbara comes into the room with the bathroom pass, he calls over to Lisa that it's her turn. Then he puts away the folders and sign-out sheets and *goes back to the book he's reading*.

When *the research group returns from the school library*, work time is over and it's time for everyone to clean up. As the class gathers for sharing, Natasha, who's in charge of the sharing session, turns to Steven first.

"How did you like your first day?" she asks.

"It was a lot of fun," Steven says, "but when do you do reading?"

"It IS reading, stupid," Derek shouts.

"You're out of order," Natasha says. "Steven, we've been 'doing reading' all day." I don't say anything as she and the others explain.

I chose this vignette for two reasons. First, it shows the possible scope of reading and writing in a classroom where the teacher understands that it's her role to involve students in a wide range of functional reading and writing and to support them in their development. Notice the range of genres that are represented. The students use reading and writing to serve the many functions of problem-solving, inquiring, engaging in functional discourse and organizing and acquiring knowledge. And as they use written language, their control over the genres develops and solidifies.

My second purpose is to show how pervasive the belief is, even among students (as Steven demonstrates), that reading in school consists of exercises, drills and prepackaged, controlled texts designed to teach reading. Many children tell researchers that even the literature they read is supposed to teach them words and skills — they know that because their grades are based on how they do on the exercises and test results, not on their actual reading. Months after school began, some of Debra Goodman's students were still incredulous that they got credit for reading at home, for instance. They had trouble letting go of the idea that reading is workbook pages.

This view of reading as instructional exercises is common not only among students, but among teachers and parents as well. "First you learn to read and then you read to learn" many educators say, suggesting that it's possible to separate learning to read from using reading for functional purposes. It explains the irony of many classrooms: children are so busy learning to read (exercises, workbook pages, vocabulary drills) that they never have time to read. In this classroom, lots of authentic reading and writing is going on.

No rat-and-pigeon learning here, no practicing of skills in isolation; instead, lots of literacy events, authentic situations in which the learners are using written language and also learning written language. At the same time, you may have noticed, the sports theme the class is working on extends into science, social studies, math, art and the rest of the curriculum.

There's a whole lot of reading and writing going on in this classroom, but what about reading and writing instruction? We see the teacher in only two events. She works with Derek who needs help with his research on the origins of soccer. She *reads with* him, *assists* him to get information from a book he can't read by himself, *demonstrates* the required style of reading for informational purposes, *encourages* him to organize what he wants to report and *takes notes* for him. Later she'll *help* him reorganize his information, but he will be the one to produce the final draft of the report and share it with the class.

We also see her involved in the class sharing, but she's a silent participant. So is this teacher not teaching? Of course she is: she has created a classroom community of learners and, under her guidance, the students have taken responsibility for much of the ongoing organization of the class. They take turns acting as class secretary and chairing class meetings and discussions, not only relieving her of many duties but also giving them responsibility for and ownership of their classroom — and creating opportunities for many functional reading and writing activities. The students are involved in planning what they will study and how, encouraged to collaborate and help each other, and engaged in a lot of self-evaluation. They know why they're doing what they're doing, and they judge how successful they've been. What they are reading is authentic language, chosen because it serves their functional needs, so they know how well they're comprehending what they're reading.

These students control their reading and writing and research. They learn on their own, in pairs, in committees, as a whole class, and they solve their problems together. They discuss what they know and need to know, and what they've learned. In the course of a school day, they initiate and/or participate in many different kinds of reading and writing.

Much had already been done before we looked into this classroom, of course. *Centers* had been organized, *committees* established to maintain and staff them, and *rules* drafted for their use. *Systems, structure, planning, order* and *organization* were set in place to encourage literacy learning in authentic literacy events. The teacher is everywhere and nowhere. Her presence is felt in class discussions, even when she's silent: *listening, observing, evaluating, ready to speak when it's needed and useful.* There's a procedure for setting up *conferences* with her. The students know that when things go wrong she'll be there, but mostly things don't go wrong because the students are involved in and committed to their own learning. They make choices which she *monitors through charts, journals, presentations* and *kid-watching.* Like all good teachers, she has eyes in the back of her head and a sixth sense that tells her when and where she's needed.

She is a *mediator* in the Vygotskyian sense. She knows what Derek can do without her and where he needs her support — she senses his "zone of proximal development." Since the information he needs isn't found in books written for young children, without her *support and encouragement* he might give up on the book he needs. She is his *scribe* as he decides what he has learned and how he will organize what he knows, making it possible for him to produce a well-organized oral report, with notes to talk from. During the process, his competency in reading and writing has grown.

She's mediating other students as well, but more indirectly. Sharon knows that when she reaches an impasse in her reading it's time for a conference with her teacher. The group in the hallway remains on task because Julia is well prepared to mediate the experiment in the teacher's place.

The teacher is also the class's *curriculum director.* She *invites* the students to share books and experiences, *provides* a classroom library and other resources, *arranges* for access to the school library, *helps* them find guest speakers, *encourages* them to use each other as resources, *approves* themes, and so on.

But how, in all this activity, can we be sure that reading and writing is developing? Here is where teachers need to understand reading and writing, both the processes and how they are learned. Because this teacher understands that reading is making sense of authentic written language, she makes sure the children are engaged with real, relevant texts of all kinds. Because she understands that writing is making sense through written language, she finds opportunities not only to involve the kids in using written language but also to get them excited about it. Carol is pouring her moral outrage into her letter to the editors of *Sports Illustrated.* Her teacher will help her to edit it so it will be well received and get some response, perhaps even be printed. John and Donavan, not the easiest to keep on task, are excited about their survey and the attention they will get when they share it.

This teacher uses a number of formal and informal evaluation tools. Her students keep *portfolios* to store what they've chosen as best representing themselves. They write *objectives* for themselves and regularly *self-evaluate,* particularly before the required report card markings. They also keep *reading-response journals.* In the first month, most of them will read more pages from books of their own choice than the total number of pages in the grade-level basal the school system still mandates.

In this middle-grade class, this teacher is focussed on helping her students to extend their reading to wider ranges of genres, and on improving their competence. She recognizes that they are at very different points in their development. "Do you have any kids who don't read or write?" I once asked her. She looked at me surprised and answered, "I wouldn't let them."

First day in kindergarten

This vignette is adapted from "If the Teacher Comes Over, Pretend It's a Telescope," by Wendy Hood (Goodman, Goodman and Hood, 1989).

> Outside my kindergarten classroom stands a large painting easel covered with butcher paper. It greets the children on their first day. "Sign in, please" and "Firmen aquí" it reads at the top. I hold a fresh box of crayons out to the children as they approach. "Hi, my name is Wendy," I say to each one. "Which crayon would you like to use to write your name here?" One by one, the kids sign in, some easily, some with only a little encouragement and some very reluctantly.
>
> As the wide-eyed kindergartners move away from the easel, Terry, my instructional aide, greets them. "Can I help you find your name tag?" She watches or helps them, as needed, and then directs them to tables set with paper, pencils and crayons. "Draw a picture of anything you like," she says as they choose their seats.
>
> Outside, two children still stand, crayon in hand, looking almost as anxious as the two mothers standing close behind them. One mom leans close to her little boy. Softly, patiently she whispers as he writes: "D-a-n-i-e-l." I greet Daniel, who smiles and rushes into the room to pick out his own name tag.
>
> Tears begin to come to the eyes of the last little girl as her mother says to her in Spanish, "You remember how. Come on now: V . . ." The girl stands, sadly frozen. Mom wraps her hand around the little girl's and moves it to shape a "V." Now the tears are flowing. "That's a fine V," I say to them both. Veronica sniffles as I slip my arm around her and we walk away from her mother, away from the easel and into the room. Although there is only one name tag left, Veronica does not choose it for herself.
>
> As the kids finish their drawings, Terry and I wander about the room looking at the pictures, talking to the children and asking them to "Write that that's a truck" or whatever. Most of them do write, or pretend to write. "Read it to me," I say, and most of them do. I respond in writing: "Where is the truck going?" This is the beginning of our journal writing.

After writing my response, I ask the children if I may keep their papers, and then invite them to choose a book to read on the rug. One by one, they complete their journal pages and meander, sometimes by way of the toy areas, to the rug area and the bookshelf. When all the children are there, we put away our books and begin our group time.

So the day goes. After group time, we move to Directed Activities, followed by Choices Time, followed by supervised cleanup, followed by a final group time. When the bell rings to go home, moms, dads and various other relatives greet their excited children. "Did you like your first day of school?" they all ask in their own way. "Yes," the kids reply. "What did you do?" the proud families ask. "Play!!"

This teacher is building her kindergarten reading and writing program around two key premises:

➤ Although this is their first day in kindergarten, most of the children have already made beginnings at becoming literate. They live surrounded by print. Written language plays important roles in their family's life and their own. The bilingual children may even have some literacy development in two languages. From the beginning, her program for developing reading and writing builds on what the children already know.

➤ From the first time they step through this classroom door, the children become aware that their teacher believes they are competent learners who will learn to read and write easily and well. They are expected to read and write and they do, at their own pace and with patient encouragement from their teacher.

The story continues:

Terry gives me a knowing look as we say goodbye. After only half a day we already know a great deal about each child, because we're kid-watchers.

We have name-writing samples. We know which children can write their first names, which can approximate their names, which write letters for their names, which write letter-like characters for their names, which can probably write their names but are already afraid to be wrong at school, like Daniel. We know which ones make writing-like strokes for their names and which seem not to know what name-writing is all about.

We know the primary language of most of the kids. Did they follow what we said in English? What language did they respond to? What language did they use to say goodbye to their families? What language did they use to "read" us their journal writing? What language did they speak at group time? Did they sing along with the English or Spanish songs? And so on.

We know if they can recognize their names. Did they choose their own name tag? In some cases, we know if they read their name or if they recognized it logographically. Did they choose a name that looked like theirs? Martin reached for Maria's tag, but she wasn't fooled by either his tag or Mario's.

We know, to some extent, their previous experience with writing implements. How did they use the pencil or crayon? Did they concentrate intently on the process of making marks or were they at ease enough to enjoy an artistic endeavor? Did they pick up the pencil in a knowing way and hold it with an experienced grasp, or did it appear clumsy in their hands?

We know something about their understanding of writing. Did they write words we could read? Did they approximate the conventional spelling of a word or two? Did they write a small group of letters preceded by a consonant that is associated with the initial sound of the word they intended? Did they write groups of letters or a string of letters? Did their writing have linear directionality? Did they use letters or letter-like figures? Did they use the letters of their name selectively? Did they use geometric shapes to represent letters? Did they write a connected series of hills and valleys? Did they duplicate the original picture when asked to "write" it?

We know more about the children's understanding of writing and reading processes when we watch how readily they write or pretend to write, read or pretend to read back what they have written. Did they write eagerly in their chosen style and then insist they couldn't read? Did they say they'd forgotten what they wrote? Did they read and giggle as if they were pulling a fast one over on us, seeming to say, "Imagine, the teacher actually believes that this says something!" When they said, "I can't," what did it mean: they don't know what writing is, they're aware there are conventions to writing they don't know, or they don't know how to spell what they want to say? Or did they write in their best five-year-old invented spelling and read back what they intended to say?

We know something about their book-handling experience. We have yet to meet a new kindergartner who doesn't know what a book is. They all find the bookshelf, select books, open them and turn pages. Some leaf through before settling on one book. Some curl into cozy spots hugging their selections. Some go through many books quickly, while others savor each page. Some read stories out loud to themselves or a friend. Some find a special picture to share with someone. Most find the front cover before opening the book. The few who don't, still hold the book right side up or turn it around within a page or two. There are always one or two who plead with the nearest adult: "Read to me?"

This kindergarten year will be drenched in opportunities and invitations for the children to use reading and writing functionally. The teacher will read to them and with them, and leave many wordless picture books and predictable books within easy reach. The children will play at reading and writing in the playhouse and other centers. By the end of the year, many of them will write, using their own invented spellings, and their published books will be displayed in the publishing center. They will be reading the environmental print in their classroom and community, and reading and rereading their favorite predictable books. Some will produce letters to Grandma that she can really read (I bet she finds the invented spellings charming), and some will be accomplished enough to produce three-page stories. Some will already read Marjorie Sharmat's *Nate the Great* or Bill Martin's *The Ghost-Eye Tree* entirely on their own.

On the other hand, some will still be writing letter strings. Some won't be able to read anything more difficult than Bill Martin's *Brown Bear, Brown Bear* or Pat Hutchins' *Rosie's Walk,* and only after hearing them many times. But no matter where they are on the continuum, they will all have made progress and they will all confidently consider themselves readers and writers. And so will their teacher. She will know just how much progress each child has made, by carefully noting incidents like this:

> March 5: Veronica, the same child who wept on the first day, selected a book in the school library. She walked over to the check-out counter, picked up a fat, red pencil roped to the counter, and slowly wrote her name on the itty-bitty line on the book card. She glanced at a friend next to her and then wrote her room number, 10. This was the first time she had ever written her name on her own! She knew it was different from her prior approximations. The look on her face as she handed me the book displayed her pride. Our supportive librarian allowed me to borrow the card long enough to make three copies: one for my files, one for the librarian to share with other librarians, and one for Veronica to give to her mother — the mother who had patiently and supportively been waiting for Veronica to bloom.

Do you notice anything missing in this kindergarten? It's true — there are no readiness materials, no pre-primers or pre-pre-primers, no worksheets, no letters to be learned one a week, no out-of-context phonics drills or flash cards. This teacher is helping her students into literacy, not getting them ready for a structured reading program.

Reading for meaning

The following vignette is based on observations made by Kathryn Whitmore in Caryl Crowell's classroom at the Borton primary magnet school in Tucson, AZ, in February of 1990 (Whitmore and Crowell, 1994).

The third-grade children in the Sunshine Room are just returning from recess, out of breath and happy after playing in the February Arizona sun. Their teacher is explaining in very few words to the student teacher, Michelle, that several of the children aren't reading for meaning as strongly as she would like and therefore she has planned a cloze procedure for them.

Three activities will be occurring simultaneously in the room, she explains to the children now seated in the group meeting area. Most of the children will write stories, using a series of clues written in both Spanish and English, choosing the language they prefer to write in. As the teacher passes out materials for the English writers, she switches to Spanish to describe the Spanish experience. The children involved in this activity disperse to the tables scattered throughout the room.

The remaining children are in two groups: three English readers are gathered with Michelle as leader, and four Spanish readers are seated at a table where Caryl is poised at the chalkboard to record their experience. Both groups will complete a paragraph-long cloze procedure selected to encourage them to focus on semantic cues, and to highlight their knowledge of syntax. Eight words have been blocked out with a dark marker to make the graphophonic cues in the passage unavailable, although the length of the word and the original spacing of the text remains intact.

Ana, David, Rosario and Raymundo speak only Spanish during this work time. The text they are dealing with reads:

Me gusta _____ el jardín zoológico. Para mi es un _____ interesante. Siempre _____ los leones y los monos. Los leones parecen _____ y al mismo tiempo hermosos y valientes. Los monos son _____. Van y vienen _____ y hacen gestos chistosos. Aunque los leones y los monos son mis favoritos, me _____ también los elefantes y las jirafas. En _____ todos los animales del jardín zoológico me fascinan.

(Translation: I like _____ the zoo. For me it is _____ interesting. Always _____ the lions and the monkeys. The lions walk _____ and at the same time are beautiful and brave. The monkeys are _____. They come and go _____ and make funny gestures. Although the lions and the monkeys are my favorites, I _____ also the elephants and the giraffes. In _____ all of the animals of the zoo fascinate me.)

The group follows a repetitive process to generate ideas for filling in the covered text: they read one sentence at a time, in unison, saying "blanco" for the spaces; then the children offer words to fill in the blanks, while the teacher records their responses. In the following example for the first sentence, the group's three ideas are written in italic.

Me gusta (I like)   jugar en (to play in)   el jardín zoológico (the zoo).
                     ir al (to go to)
                     mucho (very much)

As a child offers a suggestion, the teacher reads the sentence with the new word in place, and the group decides together if the suggestion is an appropriate answer for the blank. Only answers the group agrees on are written on the chalkboard. When each of the eight blanks is done, the group reads the entire paragraph with all of the words filled in. They discuss the whole list again and decide, at this point, that some of their choices are better than others.

Many of the words become opportunities for discussion about syntax. For example, Caryl mentions that *miro, pelean, jeugan* and *viven* are all verbs — action words — and that almost any verb would make sense in the third space. She tells the children, "It's important that stories always, always, always make sense and have meaning." In keeping with her comment, she follows each of the suggestions from the children with this question to the group: "Does that make sense?" She also suggests that when they come to words they don't know in their reading, they can substitute any word that makes sense.

The cloze procedure involves this small group in discussion about language and reading, as well as about zoo animals, for a full 45 minutes, until preparations for lunch time bring the experience to a close.

In this session, the teacher is more directed in her teaching than she usually is, which helps us to see her philosophy of teaching reading in practice. She brings an *ad hoc* group of Spanish readers together to focus on their strategies for making sense of their reading, while the student teacher does a parallel activity with some English-speaking students.

She is explicit in her instructions and comments with regard to the reading process. But she draws the children into the process, encouraging them to think about what words make sense in the blanks. She emphasizes repeatedly the importance of reading for meaning and tells the children they should always "fill in the blank" when they don't know a word, as long as it makes sense — in other words, make good guesses and keep checking to make sure their guesses make sense. The children are familiar with the frequent question: "Does that make sense?" because she asks it often when they read to her. By pointing out the verbs, she's helping them become aware of how they use their grammar to get to meaning.

Goodman, Watson and Burke (1980) call this kind of instruction a strategy lesson: a lesson that helps learners, in a focussed group or through individual experience, to build the productive strategies they need for reading. When real texts are used, with certain words blanked out, the focus is never on specific words or language units, but on the strategies themselves. In a group cloze activity, the children can think together and thus come to realize that they can deal with unfamiliar words or phrases by focussing on making sense.

Summary

In this book, we've examined literacy always within the context of real readers and writers making sense of real texts. So I chose to present the teaching of reading through vignettes of real teachers teaching real kids in real classrooms. I focussed on the experiences the children were having as well as the roles the teachers were playing, to illustrate how what teachers know informs their teaching and is demonstrated in what the children are doing. These were real classrooms, and into real classrooms come a wide range of diverse learners who require sensitive support from their teachers: some bring serious emotional and physical problems, or other problems that make it hard for them to concentrate on learning; some misbehave. What these teachers understand is that the best — perhaps the only — way to assure optimum development for all of their students is to build on their language and literacy abilities, their experiences, their cultures, their functional needs.

These teachers are shrewd kid-watchers who are well able to appraise a kindergartner's movement into literacy, a middle-grade child's resistance to reading and writing, a Spanish speaker's first attempts at literacy in English. They know children's literature and build classroom libraries. They easily come up with the right book for the right child and provide the right amount of support. These teachers take charge of their classrooms: they use materials but don't let themselves be used by them. They design their school time: hour, day, week, month and year, to provide the maximum amount of time for their students to read and write as they learn, and to learn as they read and write. And they always respond to the diverse interests and values of their students at appropriate levels of difficulty for each learner. Their classrooms are exciting and interesting places to be in and to learn in.

I'm not suggesting that every successful teacher of literacy needs to be a super-teacher. But I am suggesting that they need to be dedicated and informed professionals. With respect to literacy, that means they need to understand reading and writing as processes, how children become effective readers and writers, how children learn language and use that language to learn. And they need to know their students so well that they can support their learning and help them to achieve all they are capable of achieving.

Bibliography

American Institute of Graphic Arts. "The Development of Passenger/Pedestrian Oriented Symbols for Use in Transportation-Related Facilities," in *Visible Language* IX.2, 1975, 180.

Brown, J., A. Marek and K. Goodman. *Annotated Bibliography of Miscue Analysis.* Occ. Papers, Program in Language and Literacy No. 16. Tucson, AZ: University of Arizona, 1995.

Clay, M. "A Syntactic Analysis of Reading Errors," in *Journal of Verbal Learning and Verbal Behavior*, 7.2, 1968, 434-438.

Ferreiro, E. and A. Teberosky. *Literacy before Schooling*, translated by Karen Goodman. Portsmouth, NH: Heinemann Educational Books, 1982.

Gollasch, F.V. "Readers' perception in detecting and processing embedded errors in meaningful text," UMI# AAC 81-07445. Tucson, AZ: University of Arizona, 1980.

Goodman, K.S. *Phonics Phacts.* Richmond Hill, ON: Scholastic Canada, 1993. Published in the United States by Heinemann.

——. "A Linguistic Study of Cues and Miscues in Reading," in *Elementary English* 42.6, 1965, 639-643.

——. "Reading: A Psycholinguistic Guessing Game," in *Journal of the Reading Specialist* 6.4, 1967, 126-135.

Goodman, K.S. and L. Bird. "A Study of Texts Used in Miscue Analysis to Study Relative Word Frequency Within Texts," in *Research in the Teaching of English* 18.2, 1983, 119-145.

Goodman, K.S. and C.L. Burke. *Theoretically Based Studies of Patterns of Miscues in Oral Reading Performance.* Final Report, Project OEG-0-9-320375-4269. Washington, DC: US Office of Education, 1973.

Goodman, K.S. and Y.M. Goodman. "Reading of American Children Whose Language Is a Stable Rural Dialect of English or a Language Other Than English." Final Report, Project NIE-C-00-3-0087. Washington, DC: US Department of HEW, National Institute of Education, 1978.

Goodman, K.S., Y.M. Goodman and W. Hood. *The Whole Language Evaluation Book.* Portsmouth, NH: Heinemann, 1989.

Goodman, Y.M. and C.L. Burke. *Reading Miscue Inventory: Procedure for Diagnosis and Evaluation.* Katonah, NY: Richard C. Owen, 1972.

Goodman, Y.M., D. Watson and C.L. Burke. *Reading Miscue Inventory: Alternative Procedures*. Katonah, NY: Richard C. Owen, 1987.

Goodman, Y.M. and S. Wilde. *Literacy Events in a Community of Young Writers*. New York: Teachers College Press, 1992.

Gray, W.S. "Principles of Method in Teaching Reading, as Derived from Scientific Investigation," in *Fourth Report of the Committee on the Economy of Time*. 18th Yearbook of the National Society for the Study of Education, Part 2, C. Seashore, ed. Chicago, IL: University of Chicago Press, 1919.

——. "Report of the National Committee on Reading," in the 24th Yearbook of the National Society for the Study of Education, Part 1, W.S. Gray, ed. Chicago, IL: University of Chicago Press, 1925.

Halliday, M. *An Introduction to Functional Grammar*. London: Edward Arnold, 1985.

——. *Learning How to Mean: Explorations in the Development of Language*. London: Edward Arnold, 1975.

Halliday, M. and R. Hasan. *Cohesion in English*. London: Longman, 1976.

Hodes, P. "A Psycholinguistic Study of Reading Miscues of Yiddish-English Bilingual Children." UMI# AAC 76-26141. Detroit, MI: Wayne State University, 1976.

Johnson, S. *A Dictionary of the English Language*, reprint. London: Times Books, 1979.

Kolers, P. "Reading Is Only Incidentally Visual," in the *Psycholinguistics and the Teaching of Reading*, K.S. Goodman and J. Fleming, editors. Newark, DE: International Reading Association, 1969.

Meek, M. *How Texts Teach What Students Learn*. Avonset, Bath: Thimble Press, 1988.

Miller, G. "The Magic Number Seven Plus or Minus Two: Some Limits on Our Capacity in Information Processing," in *Psychological Review* 63, March 1956, 81-92.

Piaget, J. and B. Imhelder. *The Psychology of the Child*. New York: Basic Books, 1969.

Powell, L.C., ed. *Poems of Walt Whitman: Leaves of Grass*. New York: Thomas Crowell, 1964.

Rose, S. *The Making of Memory*. London: Bantam Books, 1992.

Rosenblatt, L. *The Reader, The Text, The Poem*. Carbondale, IL: Southern Illinois University, 1978.

Smith, F. *Insult to Intelligence*. New York: Arbor House, 1986.

Storkerson, P. "Explicit and Implicit Graphs," in *Visible Language* 26.3 and 26.4 (summer/autumn), 424-425.

Thorndike, E. *The Teacher's Word Book*. New York: Teachers College Press, 1921.

Vygotsky, L. *Mind in Society*. Cambridge, MA: Harvard University Press, 1978.

Webster, N. *American Dictionary of the English Language*. New York: White & Sheffield, 1828.

——. *Elementary Spelling Book: being an improvement on the American Spelling Book*. Cincinnati, OH: E. Morgan & Co., 1829.

Whitmore, K. and C. Crowell. *Inventing a Classroom: Life in a Bilingual, Whole Language Learning Community*. York, ME: Stenhouse, 1994.

Reading materials used for miscue analysis

"Ah See and the Spooky House," from *On Your Mark, Take a Giant Step*, Scott Foresman.

"The Clever Turtle," from *Turtles*, Scott Foresman.

"Freddie Miller, Scientist," from *Adventures Here and There*, American Book Company.

The Little Brown Hen by Patricia Miles Martin, Thomas Y. Crowell.

"The Man Who Kept House," from *Magic and Make-believe*, Nelson Canada.

"My Brother Is a Genius," from *The ABC Adventures Now and Then*, American Book Co.

"Poison" by Raold Dahl, from *Adventures in English Literature*, Harcourt, Brace and World.

"The Royal Race," from *The Magic Word*, Macmillan.

Sancho, the Homesick Steer by Helen Rushmore, Garrard.

"Sheep Dog," by J.C. Snovall, from *Widening Focus*, Allyn and Bacon.

More books on reading and writing instruction

Atwell, N. *In the Middle: Writing, Reading, and Learning with Adolescents.* Portsmouth, NH: Heinemann, 1987.

Avery, C. . . . *And with a Light Touch.* Portsmouth, NH: Heinemann, 1993.

Barrs, M. and A. Thomas. *The Reading Book.* Portsmouth, NH: Heinemann, 1991.

Cochrane, O. *Reading, Writing and Caring.* Winnipeg, MB: Whole Language Consultants, 1984.

Cordeiro, P. *Whole Language and Content in the Upper Elementary Grades.* Katonah, NY: Richard C. Owen, 1992.

Fisher, B. *Joyful Learning: A Whole Language Kindergarten.* Portsmouth, NH: Heinemann, 1991.

——. *Thinking and Learning Together.* Portsmouth, NH: Heinemann, 1995.

Gilles, C. *Whole Language Strategies for Secondary Students.* Katonah, NY: Richard C. Owen, 1988.

Harste, J. and K. Short, with C. Burke. *Creating Classrooms for Authors and Inquirers.* Portsmouth, NH: Heinemann, 1995.

Hart-Hewins, L. and J. Wells. *Read It in the Classroom! Organizing an Interactive Language Arts Program Grades 4-9.* Portsmouth, NH: Heinemann, 1992.

Harwayne, S. *Lasting Impressions.* Portsmouth, NH: Heinemann, 1992.

Kitagawa, M. and C. *Making Connections with Writing.* Portsmouth, NH: Heinemann, 1987.

Ministry of Education, Wellington. *Reading in Junior Classes.* Katonah, NY: Richard C. Owen, 1985.

Mooney, M. *Reading To, With and By Children.* Katonah, NY: Richard C. Owen, 1990.

Newkirk, T. with P. McLure. *Listening In: Children Talk About Books (and other things).* Portsmouth, NH: Heinemann, 1992.

Rief, L. *Seeking Diversity: Language Arts with Adolescents.* Portsmouth, NH: Heinemann, 1992.

Romano, T. *Clearing the Way: Working with Teenage Writers.* Portsmouth, NH: Heinemann, 1987.

Routman, R. *Invitations: Changing as Teachers and Learners K-12.* Portsmouth, NH: Heinemann, 1994.

Short, K.G. and K.M. Pierce. *Talking about Books: Creating Literate Communities.* Portsmouth, NH: Heinemann, 1990.

Stires, S. *With Promise: Redefining Reading and Writing for "Special" Students.* Portsmouth, NH: Heinemann, 1991.

Index

PLEASE NOTE The following important terms, in their general application, appear too frequently to be indexed:

alphabet, comprehending/comprehension, convention(al), cues, English, grammar/grammatical, (language) forms, (language) functions, language (oral/written), learning, literacy/literacy event, making meaning/sense, miscues, predict(ion), reading, reading patterns/process/instruction, signs/signals, social speaking/speech act, symbols, vocabulary/wording, writing/writing process.